Surrounded by a Cloud of Witnesses

Meditations on
the Weekly Scripture Readings
by
Arkansas Women

Hebrews 12:1, 2. *Therefore, since we are surrounded by so great a cloud of witnesses, let us also lay aside every weight. . . . Let us run with perseverance the race that is set before us, looking to Jesus.*

**A Project of
Episcopal Church Women of Arkansas**

Joanna Seibert, Editor

Andrea McMillin, Artist

Editor: Joanna Seibert, M.D.
Artist: Andrea McMillin
Page Design and Typesetting: Janice Drennan

Preparation of this manuscript was funded by a grant from the Episcopal Church Women of Arkansas. Proceeds from the sale of this book will fund women's ministries in Arkansas.

Library of Congress Cataloging in Publication Data

Seibert, Joanna

Surrounded by a cloud of witnesses.

I. Episcopal Church — Arkansas, II. Title 1. Meditations. 2. Women—Prayer books and devotions—English. 3. Women—Arkansas.

BV4844.S9   248.34   94-67893

ISBN: 0-914546-94-5

DEDICATION

We dedicate our writings to the "cloud of women witnesses" before us: Some wrote, some wanted to write and some taught us how to write. We will never know the names of many, but their influence on our lives through generations is very much a part of us. We especially give thanks for the ministry of Dodi Horne, who has taught many women in this book how to write from the spirit.

Proceeds from sale of this book will be used to develop women's ministries in the Episcopal Diocese of Arkansas.

PREFACE

This book is a meditative response by 66 Arkansas women to the Sunday scripture readings for the next three-year cycle: Year C (1994-95), Year A (1995-96) and Year B (1996-1997). These common scripture readings are used in the Episcopal, Catholic, Lutheran, Methodist, United Church of Christ, Christian, Presbyterian and other churches. Included are meditations for each day of Holy Week, the Holy Days of All Saints, Ash Wednesday and Epiphany. The readings include a psalm, an Old Testament lesson, a reading from one of Paul's letters and a reading from one of the gospels. Most writers have chosen to respond to one passage from one of the assigned readings. The text chosen is from the Revised Standard Version of the Bible or the New Revised Standard Version unless otherwise noted. In the Episcopal Church the readings are used for the Sunday Eucharist, mass, or communion service and have been selected according to "The Lectionary" of *The Book of Common Prayer*. The project was sponsored by the Episcopal Church Women of Arkansas. It is designed to be used each week in preparation for the Sunday service.

Several authors have referred to terms which may be less familiar to members of some denominations. *Education for Ministry (EFM)* refers to a four-year study program in the Episcopal Church, taught in small groups through the School of Theology of the University of the South at Sewanee, Tennessee. It is an equivalent to a first-year seminary course in Old and New Testament and church history. *Cursillo* is a program in the Catholic and Episcopal churches for renewal, in which participants take a "short course in Christianity" at a weekend retreat and then participate in a sustained program when they return home. *Kairos* is the Cursillo movement as a prison ministry. *Disciples of Christ in Community (DOCC)* is a study program started by John Stone Jenkins and now administrated by the University of the South at Sewanee to develop Christian community in local congregations. *The Hymnal 1982*, published by the Church Hymnal Corporation, is the book of hymns and service music used in Episcopal services. *The Book of Common Prayer*, published by the Oxford University Press, is the prayer book used in Episcopal services. *Forward, Day by Day* is a daily devotional published by the Forward Movement Press. It contains meditative responses to the daily lectionary. *ECW* is the Episcopal Church Women.

OUR STORY

John 4:1-42. It was about noon. A Samaritan woman came to draw water, and Jesus said to her, "Give me a drink. . . . Everyone who drinks of this water will be thirsty again, but those who drink of the water that I will give them will never be thirsty." . . . The woman said, "Sir, give me this water." . . . Jesus said, "Go call your husband, and come back." The woman said to him, "I have no husband." . . . Jesus said to her, "You are right. . . . What you have said is true!"

The woman said to him, "I know that Messiah is coming. When He comes, He will proclaim all things to us." Jesus said to her, " I am He, the one who is speaking to you." . . . Then His disciples came. They were astonished that He was speaking with a woman. . . . The woman left her water jar and went back to the city. She said to the people, "Come and see a man who told me everything I have ever done! He cannot be the Messiah, can He?"

Many Samaritans from that city believed in Him because of the woman's testimony . . . and many more believed because of His Word. They said to the woman, "It is no longer because of what you said that we believe, for we have heard for ourselves, and we know that this is truly the savior of the world."

Sixty-six women have gone to the well to get water. They were unexpectedly met by the Christ. They asked for the "gushing spring" water that would keep them from being thirsty again. They confessed to Him who they were. He acknowledged them. To the later astonishment of many, He then first revealed Himself to them as the Christ. They now have gone out and shared their stories with you and left the jars at the well.

WOMEN'S WRITING

I wish I could find words to tell how helping to write these meditations has changed my life. For me it has been a lesson in what may happen when I turn even a little of a project over to God for guidance. This book did not start out to be what it has become. Many people along the way molded, painted and rerouted it. There were many signs to let us know that this was a path we should be on, more than any other "project" on which I have worked.

I first heard the words "surrounded by a cloud of witnesses" in October of 1982 at Martha Lyford's funeral. These were the words beginning the funeral liturgy. The tragic death of a dear friend was only lived through by the community of witnesses who were there on that journey with her. I first knew there how God calls, supports and loves us in community.

I knew that for me writing was my best form of prayer. Could it be for others as well? I wrote for *Forward, Day by Day* two years ago. Taking time to be quiet, trying to listen to what God might be saying was *Forward's* gift to me. I have difficulty doing this "on my own." I seem to need an "assignment." Was this true for others? Could we use the same format of *Forward* for the Sunday and Holy Day Eucharist?

Our first plan was that this would be an Episcopal church women's workbook, written by Episcopal women. Then it became clear that we should hear from other women in other denominations. We have so much to learn from our different journeys. We expanded our network to Arkansas women. Hopefully we later can widen this circle even more! Our image of God can only become larger and clearer as we listen, hear, see and taste what has been revealed to others.

When I initially wrote to women about responding in meditation to the Sunday Bible readings, I had phone calls from many who were overjoyed to be asked to write. They spoke of diaries, years of keeping journals and how they longed to share some of their writings but did not know how or where. Linda Walker sent me other pieces she had written. I heard from so many who wanted to write but were afraid that their offering would not be acceptable. So many seemed afraid of failure. Then I received what they had written. It was so powerful, and they had no idea. Why do so many women not know the power of their gift inside?

Many women called or wrote that they would "try" to do the writing. They wanted to write but were having difficulty finding time. I wanted to say that finding time would be their greatest gift to themselves. I also was amazed that so many other women found their lives crowded for time.

Has it always been this way? Was there a time when women were not so busy? Is busyness an addictive disease of our culture? Is it another drug that temporarily prevents us from dealing with, knowing or feeling the pain of real life? Does it also keep us from the joy of the communication to which God is calling us?

I knew writing was not God's only way of communicating with us. I knew this might not be everyone's gift. Some hear better by writing; some, by painting, making music or listening to dreams; others, by walking, action or by . . . so many ways to hear God, so many of which I am not aware. This has been an exercise in only one method.

At first when women called or wrote that this was not their gift, I became anxious. How would I find others? Had this turned into another of my "big" projects that was more than I could handle and would consume me? One weekend late into the project I heard negatively from three women. I became depressed. That night I received a call from Ginger Crisp, a woman in Fayetteville whom I had never met. She had been referred by a friend. She called to say she was sorry she had waited so long to respond but enthusiastically wanted to do the writing and had three other friends who also wanted very much to write! The next day I received a thick letter from Sammye Dewoody. I knew she must be returning my letter and saying this was not right for her, but I opened the letter to find her first two meditations! They were so beautiful.

As our deadline drew near, I spoke to several women who said, "I just can't do this. I am sorry I did not call sooner. This is not me." I began to panic. Then I received extra meditations from Kaki Roberts and Sydney Murphy. Nyna Keeton called and mentioned she would love to do extra meditations and gave me names of two wonderful women she knew who could write on short notice. Two weeks before the deadline I was daily flooded with inspiration for responses to scripture. I wrote them down, not knowing what to do with them, for I had not assigned myself any lessons. All but two matched with readings that women called in later that they could not do!

As writings came in from so many other women, I realized I had been given sacred material—women's inner communications with God. Like so many women who first responded, I became aware that I was not worthy of the task I had been assigned. How could I ensure that these precious writings and Andrea's passionate drawings would be shared and cared for in the most loving manner and reach others who also would benefit from them? I truly started a task that proved larger than my talents. I was awed by each new writing.

This book would never have been actually published without the love, care and constant support of some other special "witnesses": Kaki Roberts, Karen McClard and Shellie Bailey from the Episcopal Church Women Board; my secretary, Rochelle Graves; Janice Drennan of The Write Stuff; and Gale Stewart of Rose Publishing.

I now want to share with you the personal communications from 66 other women from Arkansas in their response to the readings in preparation for the Sunday service. May this offering be a gift to you as it has been to us. May what has been revealed open even more doors for you. May you know and feel that you too are surrounded by a cloud of witnesses, who daily support, pray and walk with you on this journey. May you feel their presence as you sit and read these meditations weekly with women across our country, some of whom you may know, many you may not know. We are connected. We are not alone on this journey.

Joanna Seibert

TABLE OF CONTENTS

YEAR A (1995-1996)

YEAR C
1994-1995

...PURIFY OUR CONSCIENCE ALMIGHTY GOD BY YOUR DAILY VISITATION, THAT YOUR SON JESUS CHRIST

AT HIS COMING MAY FIND IN US A MANSION PREPARED

FOR HIMSELF; WHO LIVES AND REIGNS WITH YOU IN THE UNITY OF THE HOLY SPIRIT, ONE GOD —

Advent 1, Year C

Psalm 50. *The Mighty One, God the Lord, speaks and summons the earth from the rising of the sun to its setting.*

"Not by might nor by power of the sword but by my spirit says the Lord," says the gospel hymn, "Lay My Burdens Down By the Riverside." So many spiritual songs have their basis in scripture, especially the psalms.

What might or power do you covet? What might or power do you fear? Are you like I am—striving and exhausting individual resources in the struggle of gain or avoidance until you hit a wall of relieved realization? "Not by my might or the power of any one sword, but by my spirit says the Lord." Then we can let go and trust.

Lord, help us to trust. Glory to the father and the mother. Glory to the daughter and the son. As it was in the beginning, is now and ever shall be. World without end, amen, amen, amen.

I do not have to preserve a world of my invention.

Zechariah 14:4-9; I Thessalonians 3:9-13; Luke 21:25-31

Dodi Walton Horne

Advent 2, Year C

Philippians 1:1-11. *I thank my God every time I remember you, constantly praying with joy in everyone of my prayers for all of you.*

Alexandra Christine Smith was 10 days old before I could get to Louisville to visit her. I was almost overcome with impatience during those 10 days, so eager was I to give this little girl a great-grandmother's welcome to the world!

Since the announcement of her conception, I had prayed fervently for her and for her mother and father. And she was here! A miniature human being—a wee, baby girl!

When I took this absolutely perfect, tiny baby into my arms, our bonding had long since occurred. Through the constant prayers of thanksgiving for her conception and petitions for her well-being as she grew in her mother's womb, Great-Grandmother and this first, tiny great-grandchild were bonded in a Spirit of Love.

As I gazed at this minute miracle of God's grace, my heart and my eyes filled and spilled over. The tiny baby girl, Alexandra Christine Smith, gazed back into my eyes as if to say, "So this is the one who has carried me so often to Mother God's throne!"

Alexandra is the first child that I have prayed for from conception. What a bond develops through prayer! What a relationship of love develops in God's Kingdom as we lift in prayer an unborn child to our Heavenly Mother of all Mothers!

**Pray for unborn children and continue
after they come into the world.**

Baruch 5:1-9; Psalm 126; Luke 3:1-6

Nyna Keeton

Advent 3, Year C

Zephaniah 3:14-20. *Sing and shout for joy!* **Philippians 4:4-9.** *I say it again, Rejoice!*
Psalm 85. *Love and faithfulness will meet, Righteousness and Peace will kiss each other.*
Luke 3:7-18. *John preached the Good News to the people and urged them to change their ways.*

If you know J. S. Bach's "Christmas Oratorio," you have experienced the intense joy that pervades this music of a devout and inspired composer—even the Advent hymn that says, "On Jordan's bank the Baptist's cry announces that the Lord is nigh; awake and hearken, for he brings glad tidings (of the King of kings)" (*The Hymnal*, 1982, No. 76).

So our readings to prepare for this Sunday feast encourage an optimism, an intense awaiting for something much anticipated and deeply spiritual to happen—and soon. The readings show forgiveness ("I will bring the exiles home, take away your disgrace, turn shame to honor.") and practical advice ("Show a gentle attitude toward everyone, fill your minds with what is true, noble, right, pure, honorable and lovely."). Even John, who begins, "You snakes, God can make these rocks [and there are plenty there by the Jordan] into descendants for Abraham," ends with specific advice: "If you have food, share it. If you have two shirts, give one away to the person with none."

Jesus said, "Peace I leave with you; my peace I give to you."

As Paul said, "Christ Jesus is our righteousness." In Christ Jesus, righteousness and peace have kissed each other.

Make a gift to our Lord Jesus Christ: In this Advent, take an hour or a day to give your talents and gifts to an agency or organization that needs a hand to give help to those who live in darkness.

Anne Fulk

Advent 4, Year C

Luke 1:39-49. *And Elizabeth was filled with the Holy Spirit and exclaimed with a loud cry, "Blessed are you among women and blessed is the fruit of your womb."*

Whenever I read this passage, it reminds me of my own pregnancies and the women friends with whom I shared creation journeys as we studied Lamaze, ate correctly or incorrectly as the cravings led us, walked endlessly and worried about birth defects or heartburn. Some of us held each other and shed tears as pregnancies ended senselessly and with pain. During the nine months of introspection and education ran an undercurrent of awe and faith as we, together with our mates, participated in the mystery of creation and birth.

Pregnancy is one of the only times in our lives in which we knowingly participate in creation. We work with the Holy Spirit to bring life to a new being. We, like Elizabeth, mirror for our sisters the excitement and mystery. We, like Mary, say *yes* to the mystery of creation, birth and unconditional love from God.

This week read and sing Hymn 265, "The Angel Gabriel
From Heaven Came," (*The Hymnal*, 1982).
Reflect about women in your life with whom
you have shared your spiritual and creation journeys.
Write a note or two in gratitude.

Psalm 80; Micah 5:2-4; Hebrews 10:5-10

Pan Adams

Christmas Day, Year C

The Collect. *Almighty God, you have given your Son to take our nature upon him, and to be born of a [woman]: Grant that we, who have been born again and made your children, be renewed daily by your Holy Spirit.*

Human birth, children, men and women, rebirth. How do these Christmas cogitations speak to my heart? What did I spend Advent expecting anyway? A baby!!? Actually, I think this may be a possibility. To birth a child, to be a child, to love a child, to feed a child—Ah, the grace and mystery of it all! How disrespected children are in the world in which we live—we children, all children. The world doesn't believe in its childlikeness. The world exploits its children, abuses, kills its children. Does this self-destructive behavior signify a desperate need to destroy our own powerlessness, dependence?

Christmas offers us all, men and women, the possibility of experiencing a child being reconceived within us and our being reborn in childlikeness again and again throughout all eternity.

Invite your own child-within, as you remember her/him at Christmas, to come be with you for a moment and experience the wonder and joy that is possible for you.

Psalm 96; Isaiah 9:2-4, 6-7; Titus 2:11-14; Luke 2:1-14, (15-20)

Merry Helen Hedges

First Sunday After Christmas, Year C

Isaiah 61:10-62:3. *And you shall be called by a new name which the mouth of the Lord will give.*

The past one and a half years have been ones of growth and change for me. These new paths have not been easy. For the first time in my entire life, I have had to live alone. I have undertaken a course of study which has returned to my life many things I thought I had left behind forever, such as exams, papers and math. The rhythms of my every day have shifted to new priorities. I have experienced pain, and through that pain I have gained a new understanding of who I am and of the purpose of living.

God has called me to a new life (a new name)—a life I would never have voluntarily chosen. I still sometimes think that this is really not happening to me. However, I know that my new name has come from the mouth of the Lord. I have felt His presence and gentle guidance throughout these months. The pain has led to moments of joy and insights into what and who I can become.

Are you at a turning point in your life? Is there a new name waiting for you around the next turn? Whatever comes, trust the Lord of the new name. He will see you through.

Psalm 147; Galatians 3:23-25, 4:4-7; John 1:1-18

Sandy Finkbeiner

ALMIGHTY GOD, YOU HAVE POURED UPON US THE NEW LIGHT OF YOUR

ENKINDLED IN OUR HEARTS, MAY SHINE FORTH IN OUR LIVES. AMEN.

INCARNATE WORD: GRANT THAT THIS LIGHT,

Epiphany, Year C

Isaiah 60:1-6, 9.

Arise, shine for your light has come
And the glory of the Lord has risen upon you
. . . but the Lord will arise upon you
and His glory will be seen upon you.

And in rising and shining we manifest His glory.
The Lord's light is visible in me when I arise and shine.
Arising and shining have to do with being there.
Being fully present and fully ourselves.
Glowing with the light and life of a creature fully and completely alive and
   in its skin.
When I am truly present to the Truly Present One and am fully alive to
   the creation, I shine.
I radiate joy and life and light.
Arise, shine means standing—fully exposed—at the top of the hill with
your light shining for the world to see, to see the glory of the Lord.
It means being radiantly alive.
Not shrinking back in shame or fear.
It means living in the power of that light.
That light which warms and enlightens all that it touches.

In Him was life, and the life was the light of men. And the light
shines in the darkness and darkness has not overcome it.

I think of Maundy Thursday, when all the lights are extinguished.
And then one lone, brave candle pierces the blackness. It is no longer
dark. That light arises and shines.
   For the Light has come.
   Is come.
   Will come.

Psalm 72; Ephesians 3:1-12; Matthew 2:1-12

Linda Walker

Epiphany 1, Year C

Isaiah 42:1-9. *Here is my servant, whom I uphold, my chosen, in whom my soul delights.*

"In whom my soul delights" and "with you I am well pleased" are words from Isaiah and Luke that I confess I long to hear from God. Being one who is too often motivated by pleasing others—pleasing God fundamentally, pleasing my family, friends and even strangers on a more everyday level—I'm particularly susceptible to Peter's words of doing "what is right" and therefore acceptable to God. But maybe that's the catch. If *doing* right is what it's all about, then how can we explain the crucifixion of Jesus, the anointed One, the sinless One, the chosen One? Surely He did "what is right" more than anything that I could ever match.

And so, when I rethink this *doing* business, I'm struck with how backward it is. When I know that God loves me unconditionally—no matter what, in spite of myself—then doing right becomes my *response*. What I do doesn't cause God to love me. Rather, because I'm thankful that God loves me, it follows that what I do will be right in relationship to God and to others. My actions are the result, not the cause. It's what the mystics teach about *being* instead of *doing*.

It took Jesus to teach us this lesson. The Old Testament, being based on the Law, could only teach us the *doing* part. But Jesus illustrates for us how God is already pleased with us and is delighted with us. Now, here's the second catch. Just because God loves us, we will not be immune from what we don't want from life—Jesus *was* crucified. But the story doesn't end there. There is Easter; there is resurrection, that ultimate love act by God. And so, when my life presents me with crucifixion (those little deaths to my ego), Jesus is there to remind me that new birth is available for God's beloved, with whom God is well pleased.

Psalm 89:20-29; Acts 10:34-38; Luke 3:15-16, 21-22

Deb Meisch

Epiphany 2, Year C

I Corinthians 12:1-11. *Now there are varieties of gifts but the same spirit.*

The purpose of our gifts is to strengthen and make possible Christian community. If we are not a member of the community, our gift is lost. We lose the benefit of others' gifts, and the community loses the benefit of our gift. I know that my gift is needed by my Christian community, and I also know that I certainly need the gifts others offer to me through my Christian community.

But there are dangers that we need to be aware of in these spiritual gifts. One is when we assume that our gift is one that everyone should have. A gift may be public and visible or quiet and private. Another danger is when we assume that "my gift" is more important that "your gift." Our gifts are not mine and yours but His. We did nothing to merit them; so we deserve no credit for having them, only for using the gifts to the best of our ability. The gifts are His.

As members of a Christian community, it is our responsibility to see that everyone has the opportunity to exercise her gift and to see that we individually offer our gifts to our community.

Pray that we may open ourselves to God as a channel for His use and follow the guidance of the Holy Spirit.

Psalm 96:1-10; Isaiah 62:1-5; John 2:1-11

Sammye Dewoody

Epiphany 3, Year C

I Corinthians 12:12-27. *Now you are Christ's body, and individually members of it.*

November 3, 1991, All Saints' Day. The first service of our mission church, St. Margaret's. How did it happen that I was sitting in the Market Street Bargain Cinema that day? I remember seeking a church home for about five years, resting at a few places a few months before continuing the search, feeling relieved many Sundays that no one would know whether or not I was at church. Close ties might mean invasion. After living in a small town, it was kind of nice having people not know my every move.

One work day in spring '91, I got sick. What's this? In bed reading a newspaper? No one else in the house? Why I am reading the section on religion? That blasted hollow pit somewhere deep inside me keeps echoing, "Go home, go home, go home." Yes, but where? A new Episcopal church? Closer to home. A young priest, about my age, named Christoph Keller . . . must have left off the *er*. A number to call. A question-and-answer session at Charlotte's house. My mother's name is Charlotte. A foundations class, a telephone campaign—boy, if I have to do this, God had better be calling me home.

There was leadership training, small group study, personal hardships—and strangers. Yet every time I decided to go astray, the shepherd of this flock, this person with the missing *er,* would beckon. More? A call from one of those strangers? Joanna? Play the flute with you? Lillian? You want to talk about parenting on Monday nights? Joyce? You came to see *me* in outpatient? Please tell Yvonne I need her in room 504. Nancy? She needs to talk? Sunday School class? Six people here to learn with *me*? Disciples of Christ in Community? A retreat?

Yes, Lord, you have brought *me* home to people who care about *me,* who need *me,* whom I need, whom I love. They are my *family.* When one of us feels pain, it is systemic, for we are your body, dear Christ, one for all and all for one.

**Pray to help *us* remember that Jes*us* accepts *us* all
as living members of His body.**

Psalm 113; Nehemiah 8:2-10; Luke 14-21

Scottie Healy

Epiphany 4, Year C

Jeremiah 1:4-10. *Fear none of them, for I am with you and will keep you safe.*

Just as they were for Jeremiah in this passage, the most comforting words in the Bible for me are God's promise that He will be with me. It is reiterated in the New Testament in Jesus' words: "Lo, I am with you always."

When I am deeply troubled—a sick child, a family fallout, a bitter disappointment—I try to remember this promise and to couple it with the knowledge that Jesus in His lifetime on earth experienced all our human pain—physical torment as well as mental—ridicule, sorrow, disappointment, uncertainty, even death. And having been there, He will guide me through this situation and help me to cope.

It seems to me that we can follow His example by being there for others when they need us. This might mean just listening to a lonely, older person; encouraging a friend in her disappointment; a phone call, a note, an invitation to a meal or to take a walk.

And if I've been through a similar situation, I have a special obligation to help. That's why Al-Anon and Alcoholics Anonymous have been so successful. Nine years ago I had a mastectomy, took chemotherapy and survived. So when I hear of someone who has had this operation, I try to call her and offer reassurance and support.

No wonder the 23rd Psalm is read at funerals. What greater comfort than "I will fear no evil, for thou art with me"?

This week, before you pray, say this: "God's light surrounds me; His love enfolds me; His spirit watches over me. Wherever I am, God is."

Psalm 71:1-17; I Corinthians 14:12b-20; Luke 4:21-32

Betty Rowland

Epiphany 5, Year C

Luke 5:1-11. *Put out into the deep water and let down your nets. . . .*

Like Gideon, Paul and Peter in these lessons, I often have good excuses for not always doing what God calls me to do. "My clan is the weakest; my family is dysfunctional; I've tried it before, and it didn't work; I got a late start on my life; I'm too old to start something new now; the problem (of loneliness, of AIDS, of moving, of a bad marriage) is too difficult for me to deal with; others may get hurt if I do this," etc.

Years ago I read these wise words written by a woman: "Desire and longing are the whips of God." Looking back on my life, I can see that God has always called me through the deepest desires and longings of my heart. The call is always to be who I really am, to be honest about my own desires, to do what my heart tells me.

Sometimes I have resisted for weeks or months. I put off getting a divorce for years. I tried to ignore a desire to go on a solitary retreat for four months. I put off making changes in my office for weeks.

Like the three men in the lessons, it never fails that when I finally do follow God's call—whether it comes to me from my intuition or from the words of others, in my dreams or in my prayers—when I begin to speak it out loud, face the plans, face the fears, I too am given all the grace I need to face the frustration of not knowing the outcome for a while; but God always makes "a path for my steps." Sometimes immediately or sometimes when I look back after months or years, but always there comes a time when I "see the angel." I know I've caught "the boatful of fish;" I "know the peace."

The readings for this week help me remember that the cycle of call, resistance and response has always been a part of my life and my religious ancestors' lives. Grace works through this process.

Lord, I want to follow your call, to be the woman you created me to be. Help me to listen to my own desires and longings today and trust in your grace as I live my calling.

Psalm 85; Judges 6:11-24a; I Corinthians 15:1-11

Trudy James

Epiphany 6, Year C

Jeremiah 17:5-10. *Blessed are those who trust in the Lord.*

I am writing this in mid-Advent. As usual, I am in conflict, trying to make a quiet place for the Christ Child to be born anew in me, and all the while I am busily cleaning, cooking, partying, ordering, decorating, shopping, wrapping, writing and trying to "get ready."

This year, there is a new element in our life: a precious grandson. It is such a delight to watch him discover the world. All things are firsts, magic and wonderful. We know that this probably will be his only noncommercial Christmas. We want him to experience everything, to HAVE everything.

In the Psalm and Jeremiah passages we learn that those who delight and trust in the Lord are like trees planted by streams of water, strong and prospering in all they do. So it is not the experiencing and having that are of primary importance; it is the putting down of strong roots into the knowledge and love of God. This says a lot to me about the way I keep Advent, Epiphany and soon, Lent. It also says a lot to me about my grandson. I can give him things, help him experience things, but I cannot *teach* him the wonders of God. He will learn of those wonders from me only when I am so saturated that I overflow with the knowledge and love of God.

Spend some time drawing close to God, opening yourself to God, sensing how eager God is to fill you with His knowledge and love. Say a prayer of thanksgiving.

Psalm 1; I Corinthians 15:12:20; Luke 6:17-26

Madge Brown

Epiphany 7, Year C

Luke 6:27-38. *Do good, and lend, expecting nothing in return; and your reward will be great.*

Doing good has seldom been a problem for me. I often do for others, but many times I act from a sense of duty, perhaps hoping for future reward, not present joy. In the process, I miss the blessing and reward there for me at the moment.

In my role as training director for a multistate program, I can get caught up in the mundane details of my job. Recently I noticed that an elderly lady's name was misspelled on her graduation certificate from our program. Corrections had to be done at a copy center and then signed by three persons—trouble, trouble. Trying not to be demanding on support staff in another state, I decided we could mail her a corrected certificate the next week.

During the following night, I awakened suddenly from my sleep with a distinct message from *God knows where* that I should get a certificate done for her. I immediately got up and prepared a computer copy in my motel room, and the next morning I caused all sorts of extra work for myself and others to complete the job. All of us were grumbling.

At graduation the next day, when she got her certificate, she asked to make an announcement. She said that at age 73, she was receiving her very first graduation certificate. She tearfully expressed her joy, gratitude and pride of accomplishment. There was not a dry eye in the house.

Little did I imagine that preparing a certificate could be such an important milestone for her and for me. Thank you, God, for allowing me to be a part of this wondrous moment.

Pray to hear God's messages to you.
Ask for the ability to recognize and enjoy
the rewards you receive while serving others in His name.

Psalm 37:1-18; Genesis 45:3-11, 21-28; I Corinthians 15:35-38, 42-50

Dean McMillin

Epiphany 8, Year C

Psalm 92. *It is good to give thanks to the Lord, to sing praises to thy name, O Most High.*

As I read Psalm 92, my thoughts are of God's goodness and blessings in my own life. I am 52. I sew; I garden. My children are grown; my husband is retired and home *all day!*

Sounds pretty good, doesn't it? Well, let me tell you something—it is really good! I awaken every morning and say, "Thank you, God; I didn't know it was going to be this good."

I believe what makes it good is an attitude of gratitude, which is a result of discipline, acceptance and faith. I can't of my own volition assume that attitude, but I can pray and meditate every day, accept the things I cannot change and trust God.

I have practiced these things for many years, even when I was not sincere, and now can truly echo the words of the psalmist: "At the works of thy hands I sing for joy."

Jeremiah 7:1-7; I Corinthians 15:50-58; Luke 6:39-49

Ann R. Gornatti

DEAR GOD YOU KNOW WE HAVE NO POWER IN OURSELVES TO HELP OURSELVES KEEP US BOTH OUTWARDLY IN OUR BODIES AND INWARDLY IN OUR SOULS, THAT WE MAY BE DEFENDED FROM ALL ADVERSITIES THAT MAY HAPPEN TO THE BODY, AND FROM EVIL THOUGHTS WHICH MAY ASSAULT THE SOUL.

Ash Wednesday, Year C

Book of Common Prayer, page 265. *Remember that you are but dust, and to dust you shall return.*

As we kneel or stand at the altar rail on Ash Wednesday, the priest stands before each of us and marks our forehead with ashes in the sign of the cross. This marking of our foreheads with ashes reminds me of another marking of our foreheads with the cross. This other marking is done at our baptism with oil. At our baptism, the words that go with the marking are "[Our name], you are sealed by the Holy Spirit in baptism and marked as Christ's own forever." Two markings, two signs of the cross on our foreheads, one with ashes, one with oil, both marking us as belonging to God.

The marking of the cross with oil at baptism gives us a new life in Christ. The marking of the cross with ashes on Ash Wednesday points to our death, which also leads to new life. Both markings assure us that we are God's and our lives belong to God and our deaths belong to God.

Both markings assure us that our ultimate destiny is union with God. Ashes and oil. Oil and ashes. Oil mingled with ashes. We are marked with the sign of the cross. We are Christ's forever. Amen.

Joel 2:1-2, 12-17; II Corinthians 5:20b-6:10; Matthew 6:1-6, 16-21; Psalm 103:8-14

Peggy Hays

Lent 1, Year C

Psalm 91. *You who live in the shelter of the Most High, who abide in the shadow of the Almighty, will say to the Lord, "He is my refuge and my fortress, my God, in whom I trust."*

The homemaker part of me wants to strive to make our home a comfortable, refreshing refuge. Our government strives to protect its citizens. Our churches strive to be a refuge from pressures of the world. Drugs, violence, abuse, prejudice, greed and peer pressure are only a few of the monsters facing humanity today; so the goal of providing a safe haven is indeed a worthy one. Yet because of the imperfections of humans, no one endeavor is totally successful. In spite of my best intentions, my finances limit my home and its furnishings; I have forgotten to attend school functions; I have been unloving in my demeanor. Crime seems to be escalating; innocent people do go to jail; people are homeless. Our churches fail to visit the sick; ministers appear insensitive; people are overlooked; and church members continue to "sin."

Are we hypocrites then? No, only imperfect. Perhaps this is a constant reminder to put our trust totally only in God. For only through Him can we accomplish our goals, and He alone truly refreshes in mind, body and spirit. I believe God sent His spirit to us with this in mind.

**Send forth your spirit Lord, that we may be renewed
as you renew the face of the earth.**

Deuteronomy 26:(1-4), 5-11, Romans 10:(5-8a), 8b-13, Luke 4:1-13

Jenny Jackson

Lent 2, Year C

Psalm 27. *What would have become of me had I not believed to see the Lord's goodness in the land of the living?*

Sometimes life seems unbearable. I'm remembering the day my divorce was final and I moved into my condominium. When the movers had gone and my last friend had closed the door, I stood there utterly alone for the first time in my life. I had gone from my original family to being married, to having children; and now there was no one. My children were grown; there was no one away on a business trip, no one away at college; no one would be coming home. All that was left was me, and I thought my heart would break.

At that point, I couldn't see that the love of God was still out there beckoning me on and was also within me to help me continue. The way I began again was by remembering each night as I went to sleep any good thing that happened to me that day, and I would be thankful. That helped me focus on my gifts instead of my losses. After a while, God blessed me with new friends, new excitement and new hope. Now I can see clearly how He is remaking me, tearing out the old, shaping up the new; and I am not afraid anymore.

Gratitude is a powerful attitude-changing drug. It is a sure antidote for the poison of self-pity. Gratitude turns what we have into enough and more. So the solution is not so much to bring about good that should be but isn't or to deal with unhappiness that shouldn't be but is. The real solution is to recognize the goodness that is when we see it.

**Today shine the healing light of gratitude
on all the circumstances of your life.**

Genesis 15:1-12, 17-18; Philippians 3:17-4:1; Luke 13:(22-30); 31-35

Phyllis Raney

Lent 3, Year C

Luke 13:1-9. *A man had a fig tree planted in his vineyard.*

Jesus used the tree and its fruit in His parables frequently. This tree was doing something wrong. Jesus was most unhappy it had borne no fruit. It was about to lose its place in the vineyard. Jesus gave it a chance to repent, though, a second chance to produce some fruit.

What must a tree do to bear fruit? What was it doing wrong? A tree must live the life obediently within itself first; the fruit is born from that. The fruit is born upon itself as evidence of the life of the tree within itself.

The better the life
the better the fruit
the better the tree.

Then the success of the tree is dependent upon those who come its way. It rests with those who cross its path and decide whether to eat of the fruit of the tree, the fruit of its labor, obedience and life. It has no control over where its seed is cast, whether anyone will come its way, or whether anyone will eat of its fruit. The tree can do nothing about that. It is mere chance. Yet what else is there for the tree to do but live its life and bear its fruit? Life is, after all, a great chance. And who knows who might come its way and eat of its fruit—it might just be Jesus. Amen.

Plant a fruit tree. Watch it grow. Eat its fruit.

Psalm 103; Exodus 3:1-15; I Corinthians 10:1-13

Becky Tucker

Lent 4, Year C

What, Lord, are you saying to my heart? "Unto each according to what is needed." Thank you, Jesus.

What, Lord, is my response to this? "My heart sees with new eyes. I receive not what I deserve, nor that to which I feel entitled. The elder brother in me still clings to a kindergarten standard of fairness. Help me trust that my need is known and will be provided." Thank you, Jesus.

What, Lord, do you particularly want me to remember? "The will of the Father is not reducible to the logic of thought. The prayer I taught: '. . . Thy will be done.' Grandiosity drives a need to understand the Will of God. Leave it." Thank you, Jesus. Help me to leave it. Amen.

Psalm 34:1-8; Joshua 5:9-12; II Corinthians 5:17-21; Luke 15:11-32

Julia Wepfer

The prayer discipline above was taught by Jane Wolfe at Trinity Episcopal Cathedral.

Lent 5, Year C

Isaiah 43:16-21. *Remember not the former things, nor consider the things of old. Behold, I am doing a new thing; now it springs forth, do you not perceive it?*

The God I grew up with and hung around with until recently never talked this way. "I am doing a new thing!" What does that mean? You've been doing the same thing forever. I go see you on Sunday and say the same prayers and sing the same hymns and you say the same thing—nothing.

Recently I've begun to believe in the God of The New Thing—the God who says in Jesus, "Behold, I come to make all things new"—the God that Gabriel knew when he announced to Mary, "For nothing is impossible with God."

As I've altered my thoughts about who God is and how He works, I'm finding who He is and how He works is much more new and exciting than I could imagine. He's the God of surprises, of coincidences that aren't coincidence and of possibilities beyond my imagining.

All my life I've missed that about Him, and yet the evidence was there. Burning bushes that don't burn (Who would have thought of that one?), millions of frogs on a kingdom (What a way to get a king's attention. Tell me God has no sense of humor!), manna in the wilderness (What next, pennies from heaven?) and babies to old ladies and virgins. How did I miss all this?

Of course He's doing a new thing—He has been every day since the beginning of creation. No wonder He tells us not to consider the things of old. We get so focused on the past that we don't see the present, which is where new things—miraculous and amazing things—happen. If I live in the past, I can't see the present, which is the only workplace God has.

Oh Lord, teach me to be present now
and to see what new thing you do today.

Psalm 126; Philippians 3:8-14; Luke 20:9-19

Linda Walker

Palm Sunday, Year C

Luke 19:29-40. *When He had come near Bethphage and Bethany, at the place called the Mount of Olives, He sent two of the disciples. . . .*

Jesus called people to leave what they had been doing and come with him. They journeyed together as He taught them to see with new eyes and to hear with new ears. Without knowing it, they were preparing for a new life in which they would be sent out.

I never really know what is ahead. I remember when a close friend of mine was in a plane crash with six other people. He and one other survived. How near I was to Jesus through those days following that accident, trying to understand about life. How grateful I was for that friendship. How aware I was of every person I held dear. When would our shared journeys in this place end or be transformed?

Jesus sent them—*two* of them. Where does Jesus send me? I choose to respond in spite of knowing that the journey takes me to many places I do not want to go. I see what I do not want to see and hear what I do not want to hear. Why do I go? Is it because there are also celebrations of great joy, and bread to break, and a cup to share, and feet to wash? Yes, and because I know that on this journey I am never alone.

I give thanks to you, O God, for your steadfast love which endures forever.

Psalm 118:19-29; Isaiah 52:13-53:12; Luke (22:39-71), 23:1-56

Susan Payne

GRACIOUS GOD, THE COMFORT OF ALL WHO SORROW, THE STRENGTH OF ALL WHO SUFFER... LET THE CRY OF THOSE IN MISERY AND NEED COME TO YOU, THAT THEY MAY FIND YOUR MERCY PRESENT WITH THEM IN ALL THEIR AFFLICTIONS...

Monday of Holy Week, Year C

John 12:1-11. *Mary therefore took a pound of very costly genuine spike-nard ointment and anointed the feet of Jesus, and wiped His feet with her hair; and the house was filled with the fragrance of the ointment.* **Mark 14:3-9.** *She has done a good deed to Me.* (New American Standard Bible)

What a fragrant, costly sacrifice Mary made for Jesus' sake when she poured out the wonderful, soothing, fragrant, expensive ointment on His tired, dusty feet! And how He appreciated the gift she gave in serving Him!

Romans 12:1 tells me that I am to present myself, (my heart, body, soul, emotions, will) to God as a living and holy sacrifice, and that is to be my spiritual service of worship. I wonder what fragrance He smells in the divine chambers of heaven as I pour out my life to him? Is it a sweet, soothing aroma? Or is it foul-smelling, stale and unpleasant?

What does it cost me to pour out my life to Him? My all, I think, and am I willing to make that sacrifice? Am I willing to humble myself and kneel at His feet? Am I willing to give up control?

Oh, God, make me like Mary—willing to go to any expense to serve you . . . willing to stop and humbly kneel at your feet—willing to pour out all of myself before you. I pray that I could look into your face and hear you say, "She has done a good deed to me." Amen.

Psalm 36:5-10; Isaiah 42:1-9; Hebrews 11:39-12:3

Gay White

Tuesday of Holy Week, Year C

I Corinthians 1:18-31. *God chose what is foolish . . . .*

Growing up in a family of strong women and men, I learned early that "strong" was good; and "weak," bad. This was never spoken and might even have been denied, but my family's actions spoke louder: "Be strong; be good; whatever you do, do it well, even be the best if possible." I felt I never measured up. As hard as I tried, as good as I was, it wasn't quite enough, and my greatest humiliations came when I was found to be "wrong" (wrong opinion, action or answer). I felt profoundly "weak," and therefore "bad." Worse, I also assumed that *one must be strong to be loved!*

On Tuesday before Jesus went to the cross, He might have wondered at God's choice of apparent "weakness" to save the world, for He was surely a "weak reed" in the eyes of power brokers of His day. Paul says: "The message of the cross is foolishness to those who are perishing," i.e., those who rest in human power and influence. This ultimate trust of human strength is the essence of spiritual pride, "the sickness of the satisfied."* "God chose what is foolish in the world's eyes . . . ." (I Corinthians 1:27). Jesus did not come to "judge the world" (i.e., see who's strong or good enough), but to "save" it (*Save* means to "make whole.") through His love.

We don't have to be "strong" or "good" to be loved. *We are already loved* by the only One who can love us as we long to be loved. We can rejoice in our weakness, for when we know we are weak and needy, we are open to the power and strength of God's love and companionship. God reaches us through our weakness; and like Jesus, it is through our woundedness that we can help others. This is the "foolishness" of God, which surpasses all the world's "wisdom."

Jesus knew this on Tuesday, which gave Him the courage to endure the events of Friday. It was this "foolishness" of God that made Him a "light to the world's darkness" (John 12:46). I pray that I am never again ashamed of my times of "weakness" and "neediness," for in such I am open to know God as my dearest companion and to receive God's incredible forgiveness, love and transformation (wholeness, salvation). When we know that, we become "children of the light" to brighten the world's gloom.

Psalm 71:1-12; Isaiah 49:1-6; John 12:37-38, 42-50; Mark 11:15-19

The Sovereignty of Grace, by J. Allen Smith, p. 92

Ann W. Young

Wednesday of Holy Week, Year C

Isaiah 50:4-9a. *Morning by morning he wakens, he wakens my ear to hear as those who are taught.*

My struggle always is to listen, to listen morning by morning to the silence of my heart, that deep cave from where I feel the Spirit's breath. I don't know why this is hard for me or why I struggle against the stillness as though against an adversary; but almost always I do. Some of it is that I am hooked on busyness, on tasks completed and checked off my list. I'm good at that; I have had 60 years of practice and can tick off tasks like beads off a rosary.

And yet, I want to listen and to hear "morning by morning" as one who is taught. I like the ring of this verse, the eternal sound of it, that I could wake each morning of my life to hear the voice of the Spirit rich in my ear; and some mornings I do wake from dreams to hear that way, as one who is taught.

The Jerusalem Bible translates "those who are taught" as having "a disciple's tongue." What a sobering thought that this listening arms me with a disciple's tongue! The Latin root of the words *disciple* and *discipline* is the same: *pupil. Discipline*, however, not only means "a learning," but also implies "controlled behavior." And now the next part of the struggle becomes clear: controlling my tongue, that clicking, clacking, hasty member. And that brings me back full circle to listening again. If I am talking, instructing, beseeching, advising, how can I be listening?

Lord, teach me to listen, not only to your voice
but to the voice of my community as well.
Teach us to listen with the ears of "those who are taught."

Psalm 69:7-15, 22-23; Hebrews 9:11-15, 24-28; Matthew 26:1-5, 14-25

Connie Hollenberg

Maundy Thursday, Year C

John 13:1-15. *Having loved His own, who were in the world, He now showed them the extent of His love.*

Read the entire passage.

Have you ever washed the feet of someone you love or had your feet washed by someone who loves you? What effect did it have on you? How did you feel? I have never had the nerve to participate in this liturgical ceremony, but it has occurred to me that I have done it as a practical matter for my children. When David had cut his foot, it was necessary for me to keep it clean and change the dressing for several days. This deprived him of some of his self-sufficiency but strengthened his hope he would soon be healed. It gave me the opportunity to serve and comfort him. This was an humbling act for both of us, and yet it strengthened our love.

If our teacher and our Lord can perform this task for His disciples, how can we ever believe that we are too good to do such tasks for our families and friends? The excuse we often use is that we are human and Jesus was divine. No good! Jesus came, lived and died for us. He gave us the ultimate gift in the washing of the disciples' feet even though He knew He would be betrayed by one of them. Then He died on the cross for all of us. Can we accept that love? Can we pass that love along?

Pray that we may feel God's love and give of ourselves gladly to those who call on us. Father, help us to come to the Eucharist for strength and regeneration. Let the grace of this Holy Communion make us one body and one spirit in Christ, so that we may be able to serve the world in God's name. Amen.

Psalm 78:14-20, 20-35; Exodus 12:1-14a; I Corinthians 11:23-26, (27-32)

Mary Ware

Good Friday, Year C

Genesis 22:1-18. *"Take your son," God said, "your only son, Isaac, whom you love so much, and go to the land of Moriah. There on a mountain that I will show you, offer him as a sacrifice for me."*

The story of Abraham's sacrifice of Isaac has always troubled me in much the same way that our Lord's crucifixion has. The thought of willingly killing your own child or witnessing your son being nailed to a cross fills me with horror. Can you imagine your own horror at a time like this? God forbid that I should ever be asked to do something like that! The thought scares me to death.

But, of course, death is a part of life; and for the sake of my life in Christ, I am often asked to let go of, to sacrifice, to suffer loss. Didn't Jesus say, "She who loses her life for my sake will gain it?" Doesn't it make sense to be willing to give up something precious for the sake of something more precious? Because of Abraham's willingness to offer Isaac to God, his son is saved. Because of God's willingness to give up His son, we are saved. Through death comes more abundant life.

There are many things in life that can get in the way of our growth toward health and wholeness: envy, fear, addiction, desire, comfort, security, pride, poverty, self-rejection, pain—to name a few.

Reflect on what in your life gets in the way
of your relationship with God. What are blocks
to your loving that you may need to let go of?

Psalm 69:1-23; Hebrews 10:1-25; John (18:1-40), 19:1-37

Patsy Daggett

Holy Saturday, Year C

I Peter 4:1-8. *They think it strange that you do not plunge with them into the same flood of dissipation, and they heap abuse on you.* (Student's Bible, New International Version)

This scripture brings to mind what my cousin told me some time ago. For about 10 years, he drank heavily. He cheated on his wife, had numerous accidents and almost wrecked his life. I had been talking to him about his problem, hoping he would get some help, but to no avail. Alcoholism is hereditary in my family. I have seen family members lose valuable time with children, spouses and friends because of this. I did not want that to happen to him.

Almost two years ago, he called me. He told me that he had been in AA for about two weeks and that I was the first person in the family with whom he wanted to share this news. He hadn't even told his wife. He asked me to keep his secret until he told her. When he celebrated his first year of sobriety, he called me.

My pastor often tells us that we "can be in the world but not of the world." I listen to this intently and try to instill this into the mind of my child.

Children have a tendency to do things, and often they get in trouble. My daughter cuts up in class occasionally, and this often lands her in "time out" at school and at home. I tell her that just because the other kids are "cutting up" doesn't mean she has to participate. Sometimes I think my words fall on deaf ears. But my experience tells me that she will "listen," just as my cousin did, to someone who responds to her pain in love.

Thought: Pray for those who are having their share of problems. Remember, as you go through yours, someone is praying for you.

Psalm 130; Job 14:1-14; Matthew 27:57-66

Rochelle A. Graves

REJOICE AND SING NOW ALL THE ROUND EARTH, BRIGHT WITH A GLORIOUS SPLENDOR, FOR DARKNESS HAS BEEN VANQUISHED BY OUR ETERNAL KING REJOICE ALLELUIA REJOICE

REJOICE NOW HEAVENLY HOSTS AND CHOIRS OF ANGELS, AND LET YOUR TRUMPETS SHOUT SALVATION

GLAD NOW MOTHER CHURCH AND LET YOUR HOLY COURTS, IN RADIANT LIGHT RESOUND WITH PRAISES....

FOR THE VICTORY OF OUR MIGHTY KING. REJOICE AND BE

Easter Day, Year C

Luke 24:1-10. *And they remembered His words, and returning from the tomb they told all this to the eleven and to all the rest. Now it was Mary Magdalene and Joanna and Mary the mother of James and the other women with them who told this to the apostles. . . .*

I believe it is no small matter that it was women who first told the apostles and other followers of Christ about the empty tomb and the message of the two men. Verse 11 continues, ". . . But these words seemed to them [the disciples] an idle tale, and they did not believe them." Sound familiar?

What makes these women (and many others) so powerful is that vulnerability to allow God's power into their lives. They have recognized their own powerlessness in many situations. They have strived to live not by the power of words or logic, but by being obedient to the Word, no matter how that might conflict with the words of accepted authority.

The women went to the tomb to minister to the dead Jesus. They had little understanding of the immortality of the soul. But they were reminded that God's power is able to break human boundaries and expectations. Being reminded of what Jesus had told them provided them with a spark of understanding of what it all meant. They did not have to understand *how* it had happened. They knew it to be the truth; they demonstrated faith by telling others this truth.

Power for Christians is living in that kind of faith—faith that God's promises will be fulfilled, that the risen Christ wants to dwell within us and that we are loved, forgiven and meant to be part of God's eternal kingdom, even when we are confused, doubtful or question what God does or asks us to do. That power dwelling in us allows us to do things which others believe are impossible; that power enables us to challenge and question traditional thought. It gives us courage to leave the tomb and deadness which surrounds us and encounter the living Christ!

Find out more about women with faith so that you can learn by their example how to claim the power of the risen Christ. Share with them in proclaiming with enthusiasm, "Alleluia! The Lord is risen!"

Acts 10:34-43; Psalm 118:14-29; Colossians 3:1-4

Joyce Hardy

Easter 2, Year C

Job 42:1-6. *Then Job answered the Lord, "I know you can do all things, and that no purpose of yours can be thwarted."*

No purpose of God's can be thwarted. What comfort! What strength! What a promise!

When things are not going the way we want, we may wonder if God's purpose is being thwarted. Yet Job reassures us that no purpose of God's can be thwarted.

As we live our lives, we listen for God's purpose. We listen through our nighttime dreams, meditation, prayer, scripture, worship and countless other ways. As we seek to live according to God's purpose, help can be found in developing our inner talents and gifts. When we match our God-given talents with authentic needs in the world, doors seem to open.

What happens if doors are not opening, and they are closing instead? What if we are ill unexpectedly? What if our beloved friend is fighting for life in a battle with cancer? What if the job we're so eager for has not emerged in the way we would have expected?

In all things, God is working God's purpose.

Sometimes it's only years later when we can see that a time when we thought we were being thwarted was really a time of incubation, maturation or hibernation preceding the next phase of our lives. Sometimes in hindsight we see how the hand of God protected us by closing a door. We are grateful in hindsight.

Since God's purpose is *never* thwarted, if you are finding a closed door, you must approach it another way. Sometimes you wait. Sometimes you knock again. Sometimes you grieve and let it go and trust that another door will open. God has a plan, and this plan will not be thwarted.

**God, when we are knocking at a door, give us your discernment
to know whether we are to wait at the door, knock harder
or let it go. As others we love meet closed doors,
help us find faith in Job's words that
"no purpose of yours can ever be thwarted."**

Psalm 111; Acts 5:12a, 17-22, 25-29; John 20:19-31

Susan Sims Smith

Easter 3, Year C

John 21:1-14. *Just after daybreak, Jesus stood on the beach; but the disciples did not know that it was Jesus.*

For the last six months, I have been learning to look. My vision is fine, with the help of glasses or contact lenses. However, my training as a docent for the Arkansas Arts Center has shown me dramatically that I miss much that is directly before me. I am so much like the disciples at the sea of Tiberias. My docent training was meant to show me the ways we can introduce exhibitions to people interested in art. What I have learned, though, was that each work of art yields new discoveries every time I look. My eyes allow me to see when I am capable of understanding. But my eyes don't tell me everything. I try to appreciate abstract expressionism, but all I see are blotches, wide swaths of intense color and strange lines creating empty spaces. I look, but I cannot see. I do not understand.

So I ask Patrick, my 7-year-old son. We stand before a huge canvas where I see a woman with a shopping cart. Patrick disagrees—no, it's not just a woman. She is homeless; all her belongings are in the grocery cart and her dress is a garbage bag. She is looking right at me, but I do not see her until Patrick shows me.

We stand before another huge canvas. This one is covered with paint, textured surfaces, shadows. I see nothing. I stare and take in nothing. "See the ship," Patrick says. "Look, we're going out to sea. We can climb that white ladder to get onto the ship. There's someone standing there by that lighthouse. Mom, who is that?"

I still stare. I've just begun to make out the ship. My eyes are starting to see.

Take something common in your life and look at it carefully.
What about it is new to you? What do you look at, yet never see?
Pray that God will open your eyes.

Acts 9:1-19a; Psalm 33; Revelation 5:6-14

Teresa Luneau

Easter 4, Year C

John 10:22-30. *My sheep hear my voice and I know them, and they follow me; and I give them eternal life, and they shall never perish, and no one shall snatch them out of my hand.*

A few years ago my father died. He had heart problems for many years and suffered a severe stroke 18 months before he died; so his death was not a surprise to us.

Even though the loss was devastating to me and my family, we had the assurance and certain knowledge that we would be with him again. We knew we were still on this journey or trip, but that he was now safely home. This was so important for us because we knew he was well and healthy—no longer feeble, weak and incapacitated.

As my two sons—7 and 13 at that time—grieved, they began to remember the last months with Daddy and their conversations together. Daddy had spent time with them, telling them that he was getting weaker and soon was going to die. He shared with them his intimate friendship with Jesus, how Jesus had shown him that He would be with him, that Heaven is real and Daddy was to be there for eternity.

There was never fear on Daddy's face, only an incredible peace. Never was there anxiety in his voice, only love and real anticipation. During those last months, he refused to take oxygen to help him breathe easier. He told me then that he was ready anytime Jesus came for him and he did not want to prolong his time here any more than necessary.

I understood so much more about Heaven from Daddy. He taught us all so much. He knew the Shepherd. He had heard His voice leading him home to safety, comfort and peace. He was following that voice. By following, Daddy knew from Jesus that he would be given eternal life and there should be no fear. He was safe in Jesus' hands, and he knew it.

I miss Daddy terribly at times, but I can still smile and have joy in my heart for him and know that one day we will be together for eternity.

Pray for those who have lost a loved one recently.

Acts 13:15-16, 26-33; Numbers 27:12-23; Revelation 7:9-17; Psalm 100

Sydney Murphy

Easter 5, Year C

Leviticus 19:1-20; John 13:31-35. *Just as I have loved you, you also should love one another.*

Today's lesson is about God's rules for leading a good life (Leviticus 19:9-18) and love (John 13:34). Many times as children we are taught that these two things are related. If we are "good" at the doctor's office, we will receive a treat and our parent's favor. If we do well in school or on the job, we will be given high marks and promotions. Yet, what does one have to do with the other in the Lord's eyes?

The past two years I have had occasion to remove many of my adolescent's rewards: phone privileges, car keys, seeing friends, allowances, etc. Yet, I have always loved her; and in the general scope of things around our house, I am not convinced that the giving or retraction of these rewards influences her behavior one way or the other.

The closest I have come to imagining God's love for me is to appreciate my own love for my children. I am pleased when they are "good," but their behavior is not a conditional aspect of my feelings. In fact, I tend to love them most when they are vulnerable or faltering.

In our need for compassion, in our moments of weakness, when we are sick or when we are despondent and depressed, are the times when we are most often given insight into the magnitude of God's love. This is what I should try to emulate—to love another as God loves me. When I see another stumble, reach for his or her arm. When I see another triumph, be the first to applaud. When I see another in danger, move to assist. When I see another sick, move to be near. When another is lonely, move to comfort.

**Pray that we may be attuned to the needs of others
and that we respond in a suitable way.**

Psalm 145; Revelation 19:1, 4-9

Elaine Williams

Easter 6, Year C

Revelation 21:22-22:5. *Then the angel showed me the river of the water of life, bright as crystal flowing from the throne of God.*

I have a friend who is being consumed by her work. She thinks of nothing else. She is chronically tired, sick or exhausted. She does not have time for anything else. When I talk to her, I feel she does not have the time for conversation or I am imposing on her. Her life revolves around her work. When one of her children was sick, she said, "He can't get sick; he needs to help me with my work!"

One day I saw myself in my friend's actions. She may have even modeled her lifestyle from me. I so often get into the same mode, consumed by my work. Everything else relates to its place in relationship to what I am doing. I am not there for my family, friends or husband. They are there for my plan, my agenda. I deeply care about them but take their relationships for granted and do nothing to nurture or water it.

I seem not to be able to see my own character defects but can so clearly see them in others. God's grace is given when "I am visited by angels" and am able to see my reflection in another's defects instead of being appalled by my friend's behavior. I cannot change my friend. Is there hope that I may change? My job is to recognize this pattern in myself, confess it and pray that God will change me and that I will be receptive to the avenues He opens to me for this change. I ask for your prayers for me and my friend.

Pray that you will see, hear the angels
who will show you the river of the water of life today
through the Holy Spirit working in you or through others.

Psalm 67; Acts 14:8-18; John 14:23-29

Joanna Seibert

Easter 7, Year C

I Samuel 12:19-24. *All the people said to Samuel, "Pray to the Lord your God for your servants, so that we may not die; for we have added to all our sins the evil of demanding a king for ourselves. And Samuel said to the people, "Do not be afraid; you have done all this evil, yet do not turn aside from following the Lord, but serve the Lord with all your heart; and do not turn aside after useless things that cannot profit or save, for they are useless. . . ."*

This passage makes me think of the decade of the 1980s, what has been called the "Me Decade."

I have a good friend who settled with her husband in Dallas after he graduated from law school. A smart, talented man, he chose to work in a specialized area of tax law. He and his wife are natives of Little Rock.

A couple of years after their move, I visited them for several days. My friends had warned me that many Dallas "thirty-somethings" were extremely materialistic. A number of their friends and acquaintances lived in million-dollar homes, drove expensive foreign cars and had "live-in" nannies for their children.

More than these trappings of wealth and consumerism, I was amazed at their attitudes. Couples who, like me, had grown up in middle-class Little Rock had "gone Hollywood." They were obsessed with getting their children on waiting lists of the "right schools," taking certain kinds of vacations, driving particular brands of vehicles and, especially, living in the most exclusive neighborhoods.

It is so easy to get caught up in such attitudes, especially when everyone you know seems to share the same values. It would be untrue to say that I've never wished for an object or lifestyle that I couldn't have. It takes strength of character to recognize and "turn aside from things that cannot profit or save." Being grounded in God, Jesus Christ and the Church is the best defense.

**Pray for the vision to recognize and reject
"things that cannot profit or save."**

Psalm 68:1-20; Acts 16:16-34; Revelation 22:12-14, 16-17, 20; Acts 16:16-34; John 17:20-26

Julie Keller

THE ADVOCATE, THE HOLY SPIRIT, WHOM THE FATHER, WILL SEND IN MY NAME, WILL

TEACH YOU EVERYTHING, AND REMIND YOU OF ALL

THAT I HAVE SAID TO YOU. PEACE I LEAVE WITH YOU; MY PEACE I GIVE TO YOU.

Day of Pentecost, Year C

Joel 2:28-32. *Your sons and your daughters shall prophesy, your old men shall dream dreams, and your young men shall see visions. Even on the male and female slaves, in those days, I will pour out my spirit.*

Sons and daughters will prophesy; old men will dream dreams; young men will see visions. God will pour out spirit even on the female slave, the lowest of the lowly! What a wonderful way the Bible has of turning upside down the world's hierarchies of power. "A little child shall lead them.... The lion shall lie down with the lamb.... The last shall be first." And our question for today is, can we really let our own lives be turned upside down in a similar manner?

To whom do we listen? Whom do we follow? Whom do we emulate? The meek may be blessed, but generally it is the rich and famous who get the attention! Who gets our attention? Do we listen to the female slaves? Do we pay attention to the children? Do we hear what the poor are saying to us?

I once met a grocery clerk in a different social situation, and she said, "I remember you. You were always so good-humored when you went through the checkout line." And I thought, who else sees me when I go through the checkout line? Who else observes me when I am not trying to impress someone, when I am not on my best behavior? And what kind of messages do I send other people by my own lack of attention to what they have to say? And what visions do I miss because I haven't the time or inclination to speak to those whom the world labels *unimportant*?

Psalm 104:25-37; I Corinthians 12:4-13; John 20:19-23

Mary Donovan

Trinity, Year C

Isaiah 6:1-8. *In the year that King Uzziah died . . . I heard the voice of the Lord saying, "Whom shall I send, and who will go for us?" And I said, "Here am I; send me!"*

Wordsworth wrote:
The world is too much with us; late and soon,
Getting and spending, we lay waste our powers:
Little we see in nature is ours;
We have given our hearts away, a sordid boon.
I learned this verse from my 10th-grade English teacher, an Episcopalian. Two years later, when she learned I was disenchanted with my church, she asked me to go to church with her. "Oh no," I said, "I'll never be an Episcopalian."

We are called by God to pray, and prayer includes listening to God. We must pay closer attention to what God says because we may mistake His voice for something else. As a youth, I thought God spoke in thunder and lightening and Shakespearean English. I never heard God talk to me.

The Bible says that God speaks in ordinary ways. God spoke to Adam and Eve as they walked through the garden, to Moses as he was tending his flock on the hillside, to Gideon as he was threshing wheat, to Amos as he was pruning his vineyard, to Hosea in the clattering collapse of his marriage, to Jeremiah in the death rattle of a nation, to Matthew as he was squaring accounts at the tax table and to Peter, James and John while they were fishing. God can speak to us in church, as He did with Isaiah in the temple in the year that King Uzziah died. God can even speak to us through ordinary women trying desperately to write about extraordinary things.

God speaks to you and me. With the complexity of society, we are so busy. People and jobs fill all our time. We may look as if we have it all together; yet underneath we are lonely, anxious and despondent. We have drifted away and listen to words other than God's. We must listen for God's Word and turn to Him.

**This week take time to listen to what God is saying to you
and turn to Him.**

Psalm 29; Revelation 4:1-11; John 16:(5-11), 12-15

Kaki Roberts

Proper 6, Sunday Closest to June 15, Year C

Psalm 32:1-8. *"I will confess my transgressions to the Lord;" then thou didst forgive the guilt of my sin.*

Sometimes it seems hard to recognize our own sins. And once recognized, how deep should we go? When I kneel in church on Sunday mornings, I feel that I must confess my sins; and yet since I have not committed adultery, nor robbed a bank, nor told a monumental lie, nor dishonored my mother and father, what should I then confess to gain forgiveness?

Maybe the question should be: How shallow should we go? If we have not committed a major sin, what about the minor ones or those not even mentioned in the Ten Commandments?

What about being unkind deliberately? What about being prejudiced against those of another color or creed? What about a "Whatevergate" our business calls us to make? What about breaking the law in the knowledge we probably won't get caught?

As time has passed since Moses brought the commandments down on tablets of stone, sins not even dreamed of in his time have evolved in man. And we do not have the benefit of new stone tablets to guide us. So what shall we do to get our old and new sins forgiven?

We must not try to "put one over" on the Lord. It just won't work. Put your trust in Christ Jesus. Tell Him of your transgressions, both major and minor, both old and new, and you will be forgiven . . . and, more importantly, you will be blessed.

Count on it; you have God's word.

Pray for courage to face God with those things
we do that we ought not to do
and thank Him for the blessing of forgiveness.

II Samuel 11:26-12:10, 13-15; Galatians 2:11-21; Luke 7:36-50

Robin Sudderth

48

Proper 7, Sunday Closest to June 22, Year C

Galatians 3:23-29. *There is neither Jew nor Greek, there is neither slave nor free, there is neither male nor female; for you are all one in Christ Jesus. And if you are Christ's, then you are Abraham's offspring, heirs according to the promise.*

It would appear from this passage of Paul's letter to the Galatians that even long ago women had a rightful place in the family of Christ. But it certainly took a long time for the rest of the family to take Paul at his word.

I grew up in the Episcopal Church. As I observed my mother and her friends, their contribution to the church was limited to cooking meals for those occasions when the members met in a body to eat and Altar Guild duties, which included the housewifery tasks of cleaning silver and washing and ironing the linens used in church services. All the other church duties, were the sole province of men—the vestry, lay readers, chalice bearers, etc. The family of Christ was divided into what women did and what men did, it seemed to me. And this remained true in my adulthood.

There came a period in my life when my attendance at church dropped off to nil. Imagine my surprise when after a several-year hiatus, I returned (*joyfully, I must add*) to God and the church and found women finally and usefully had been included in the promise. Women were serving the Eucharist chalice; girls were acting as cross bearers and acolytes; women were reading the lessons; and miracle of miracles, a woman was actually serving as a priest in this particular community.

Now we must await the day on this earth when there is no longer a difference between Jew and Greek, when the words denoting slavery and freedom are no longer used to differentiate the conditions of human beings, and when all are one in Christ Jesus.

Pray that all of God's people may come to realize they are welcome to be an heir or heiress of the promise; all can be one in Christ Jesus.

Psalm 63:1-8; Zechariah 12:8-10, 13:1; Luke 9:18-24

Robin Sudderth

Proper 8, Sunday Closest to June 29, Year C

Psalm 16. *The Lord is my chosen portion and my cup; thou holdest my lot.*

The portion of this psalm that speaks most loudly to me is that which says "thou holdest my lot." I am drawn to it because it speaks to my life for today and what the future has in store for me.

I used to pray a long cafeteria list of what I wanted the Lord to do for me and for my husband, what I thought my children needed and how to provide for my friends and all those for whom we are supposed to pray. Once I had prayed for everyone else and instructed the Lord on how He should handle their lives, so to speak, I felt it was my turn; and I would pick and choose those items from the list that pertained to me and mine.

In the past year, however, I have changed my prayers from a long list of what I thought the Lord should be doing for the world, nation, state, "people," and finally me and mine to a simple prayer of acceptance of His will for my life. This has come about through my experience as a member of an intercessory prayer team. Intercessory team members receive a list of names of those for whom prayers are desired. The team does not know their needs, only that they are needful of prayer. As I go down the list of names, touching each name and calling it out, my prayer is a simple one:

Lord, for those for whom our prayers are desired, thy will be done.

Psalm 16 tells me that the Lord holds my lot in life in His hands. He holds the key to today and to all my tomorrows. So as I pray for others, I now pray for myself: Lord, let me live within the center of your will for my life.

**Pray that you and yours will live within the center
of God's will for your life.**

I Kings 19:15-16, 19-21; Galatians 5:1, 13-25; Luke 9:51-62

Robin Sudderth

Proper 9, Sunday Closest to July 6, Year C

Psalm 66. *Rejoice!*

I say the first line of a psalm when someone tells me they can't sing in church: "Make a joyful noise. God doesn't care if you're in perfect tune." As a choir member, I sing some moving pieces of music; and on some of the uplifting, upbeat songs, another member adds drums, shakers and tambourine.

All of the readings have *rejoice* as a key word. We are to rejoice because we belong to God and He will not allow harm to come to us.

I have had a rough life compared to some but not bad compared to others. God will give us no more than we can handle; rejoice. What we have coming is going to be incredible. I don't think I pay enough dues to warrant being a member of such a prestigious club, but Jesus tells His disciples in Luke, ". . . Rejoice, because your names are written in heaven."

I was baptized as an infant and believe my name has been on the slate for some time. As a child, I had friends of other denominations tell me I needed to be saved. "From what?" I would ask. I was told that because I was baptized as an infant, God wouldn't want me, it wasn't good enough. I would go home in tears. My mother tried to explain that God did want me, in fact, already had me. When I was confirmed, I thought I understood. The older I get, the more confusing things are.

With God, harm isn't supposed to come to us. One would have to define *harm*. Is it bodily injury, lack of food, shelter or friends? I think of *harm* as "a loss of spirit." I can do more to my spiritual self than to my body. No matter how bad things get, I know God is with me; so I rejoice. Bad times would be unbearable if I thought God were not with me.

If being a Christian were easy, everybody would be doing it. As it is, the world is full of nonbelievers, doubters and those who are confused. We are to rejoice for them. We are to rejoice for believers also. Who doesn't rejoice in the birth of a baby or a miraculous recovery? But we also need to rejoice for the little things. In all things, rejoice.

Think of all the little things in life and give thanks.
Pray for your enemies. Rejoice in life, family and friends.

Isaiah 66:10-16; Galatians 6:(1-10), 14-18; Luke 10:1-12, 16-20

Karen Johnson

Proper 10, Sunday Closest to July 13, Year C

Psalm 25. *Unto thee O Lord, do I lift up my soul. . . . Let me not be afraid.*

The opening lines of this psalm are special to me. They signal a time of youth and fewer worries. In my college days, I spent a lot of time at the Baptist Student Union (BSU) on the University of Central Arkansas campus—not the typical place to find cradle-born Episcopalians, but a place for Christians to be together. Episcopal students were few; most were going to Hendrix College.

While hanging out at the BSU, I met Diane, a very talented person and quite willing to teach anyone guitar. Since I was active at Camp Mitchell during the summer and working with the EYC in Conway, I grabbed the chance to learn. The first song I learned was based on this psalm. Playing it over and over was like praying. "O, my God, I trust in thee, let me not be afraid, let not my enemies triumph over me." I really wanted to become proficient at the guitar, and the constant practice enabled me to make time for prayer life. Like most college students, my time spent talking to God had been right before tests and Sunday at church—not a daily ritual.

I began to notice little changes. I became more focused in my chosen field of study, and I tolerated people I really didn't like. I seriously prayed for others—all because Diane wanted to share her wonderful talent.

I had an epiphany. I really enjoyed the rest of that semester. I learned other songs; but this psalm, set to music, stuck in my repertoire forever. I found myself questioning how to do God's will and searching to see if I was being called to something else or possibly just rediscovering my own spirituality.

I never really mastered the guitar, but I passed the joy of playing on to my younger sister. I still sing this psalm when I'm alone or in prayer, mostly to remind myself God hasn't forgotten me as I deal with life's woes and joys.

**Practice trusting all things to God this week. Share a talent.
Be a good Samaritan to someone less fortunate.
You may be the only Christ some people meet.**

Psalm 25; Deuteronomy 30:9-14; Colossians 1:1-14; Luke 10:25-37

Karen Johnson

Proper 11, Sunday Closest to July 20, Year C

Luke 10:38-42. *The Lord answered her, "Martha, Martha! You are worried and troubled over so many things, but just one is needed. Mary has chosen the right thing, and it will not be taken away from her."*

Recognize Martha, type-A personality, chairing a dozen committees, trying to save the world but needing someone to save her from herself, likely candidate for migraines, ulcers, high blood pressure or heart attack?

A friend once told me I make Martha seem like Mary. I am not close to resembling Mary, but my Martha side has eased up a bit. I still rush to clean house, top to bottom; get paperwork done; beat morning traffic. Do friends and family really care if my house is spic and span? Is my supervisor thrilled that paperwork is finished? Is beating traffic so important I ignore my husband? I should answer all these questions, *no*; but I hear my Martha saying, "Of course, all of this is important."

The '90s are a Martha decade. We have computers to speed up everything; we can take them on vacation and use them to register for classes, pay bills and check bank balances. Faxes keep us in touch with the business; modems, with the world. With the car phone, not only can we work at work, we can do it en route, at home or on vacation. Would Mary answer "Call Waiting" while speaking to Jesus? I'm afraid I might ask Jesus to hold just a minute.

Jesus tells Martha that Mary has the one thing needed—Him. After 2,000 years, one would think I would take notice. Turning everything over to God is difficult. I insist on doing things my way first. When totally at wit's end, I let go, and things work out mysteriously. If I tell someone *no*, I don't lose my friends, and I am asked to participate again.

I have to take care of me. I can't do what God has intended if I am so tired and stressed out I don't know if I am coming or going, or passing myself on the way.

Dear Heavenly Father, grant that I may find time to fully appreciate the world in which I live. Help me through this week to turn everything over to you. Let me be your instrument in the world so that I may do your will, not mine. Amen.

Psalm 15; Genesis 18:1-10a , (10b-14); Colossians 1:21-29

Karen Johnson

Proper 12, Sunday Closest to July 27, Year C

Psalm 138. *All the kings of the earth shall praise you, O, Lord.*

The responsibilities and pressures of single parenthood seemed quite overwhelming at times. I tried to keep my head on straight with four growing, active children and a full-time job. Chores were divided up and usually done willingly to the best of the children's abilities. I found myself taking for granted what was done and only commenting on what was left undone or not done to my expectations. Praise did not seem to be in my vocabulary, and I was not even aware of my shortcoming.

One day when I was assessing the kitchen cleanup job and pointing out what still needed to be done, 8-year-old Cynthia said, "When do we get to the good part, Mommy?" I knew then it was time to reassess my comments.

**Dear Lord, help us to know that in praising others
we are extolling you. For it is through our sensitivity
that we can foster your presence in others. Amen.**

Genesis 18:20-23; Colossians 2:6-15; Luke 11:1-13

Jane Roark

Proper 13, Sunday Closest to August 3, Year C

Ecclesiastes 1:12-14; 2:(1-7, 11), 18-23. *I, the teacher, when king over Israel in Jerusalem, applied my mind to seek and search out by wisdom all that is done under heaven; it is an unhappy business that God has given to human beings to be busy with. I saw all the deeds that are done under the sun, and see all is vanity and a chasing after wind.*

I have spent my afternoon waiting, waiting and testifying at a child abuse trial. The reading from Ecclesiastes perfectly describes my condition. I hate preparing and testifying with a passion. It is time-consuming and threatening. I have done this for more than 20 years, and it is only a little easier. I always feel as if I am on trial when I am on the stand. I rarely receive any feedback as to what has happened to the children immediately or in years to come. It is a difficult job with essentially no positive reinforcement. This is not what I wanted to do in the last remaining week of my sabbatical from work.

As I was driving home, however, grace and wisdom visited me. Suddenly I was overcome with the knowledge that today I had been given the "privilege" of making a real difference in someone's—specifically a child's—life. What I said and how I said it would make a real impact on that child's future. Rarely do we have the opportunity to make such a difference in the direction of someone's present or future.

I would not know the results, and she would never know me or what I had done. I was sowing seeds and would never see the harvest. This may be why this is so difficult. We often don't mind hard tasks if we know the results are productive.

My spiritual advisor has recommended that to "get out of myself," I might consider doing some anonymous "good" for others. That has been difficult for me, for I am goal and reward oriented. I think this job is what my friend is suggesting I do. I pray that God will continue to try to move me from my self-centered world of vanity.

Perform an anonymous "good deed" this week.

Psalm 49; Colossians 3:(5-11), 12-17; Luke 12:13-21

Joanna Seibert

Proper 14, Sunday Closest to August 10, Year C

Luke 12:32-40. *Have your lamps lit. . . . Blessed are those . . . whom the master finds alert when He comes.*

I have had the rare opportunity to be on sabbatical for six months. This has been my gift—having the opportunity to stay awake, alert. I spend most of my life on the edge, going from one idea or task to another, exhausted at the end of the day. During this sabbatical, I have only occasionally exhausted myself. I have not used up all of my oil. I have an exhaustive agenda for each day, but I have learned that God speaks most clearly to me in people and events that are not on my agenda. What I have planned may indeed be God's plan, but what comes into my life that is not on my agenda is often God interjecting, speaking directly to me. In the past, I would ignore and resent these intrusions. During this sabbatical, I have had time to listen to the interruptions. I cannot hear or act on them if I am so exhausted by my own agenda. I am learning to keep energy in reserve for these "new directions." My children have taught me the most about this new life. They constantly tell me about new plans, ideas and problems. If I have no oil or energy, I cannot be there when they call.

How do I keep this oil for the lamp to lighten the way? Many "12-step" friends will tell you about "halt." You are using up your reserve when you become hungry, angry, tired or lonely. When I become agitated, restless, discontented, I am usually over the edge and in one of the "halt" modes. I have gone too far, burned my oil and am running on empty. It is a sign to stop, rest, not to make any decisions.

I am aware of when I have gone too far. How do I keep from getting there? The method may be different for each of us. For me it is a daily walk, music, prayer, meditation, exercise, Eucharist, sitting outside, writing, being creative. I also have painfully learned that even when life seems too unbearable, I must stay with it, try to avoid mind-altering addictions—food, alcohol, drugs, work, power—which may temporarily relieve my pain but which keep me from being alert and available for the answer.

The Bridegroom, the Master, is here today in this moment.
Listen and wait for His call.

Psalm 33; Genesis 15:1-6; Hebrews 11:1-3, (4-7), 8-16

Joanna Seibert

Proper 15, Sunday Closest to August 17, Year C

Hebrews 12:1-7, (8-10), 11-14. *. . . But He disciplines us for our good, that we may share His holiness.*

Structure. Order. Discipline. A few months ago a spiritual guide began repeating those words to me over and over and over. At first, I threw them back with venom. Why couldn't I just keep doing things when I wanted and how I wanted? Why should I have to do anything that I didn't want to do? I was furious. Yet I knew that other people had a relationship with God that I did not have, that other people had relationships with one another that were missing from my life. Gradually the idea of structure, order and discipline began to stick, but they were not welcome. They were more like snail slime oozing down a sea wall.

It began rather simply. I made my bed every day. I went to bed at the same time every night. I got up at the same time every morning. Instead of praying on the run—if I prayed at all—I began praying at the same times every day.

Without the chaos, I could hear God. He was speaking to me. The shock. The amazement. Without the chaos, I can let God in to fill the void. That vast emptiness that is always calling for something can call for God; and the emptiness is replaced with fullness, the fullness of God's love and my desire to please Him.

**Pray for the willingness to follow God's discipline
so that you can accept His love.**

Jeremiah 23:23-29; Psalm 82; Luke 12:49-56

Pam Strickland

Proper 16, Sunday Closest to August 24, Year C

Psalm 46. *Be still, and know that I am God.*

Jump out of bed. Pray, pray, pray. Hop into the shower. Pray, pray, pray. Drive to work. Pray, pray, pray. All through the day. Pray, pray, pray. Frantically pray from dawn to dusk.

That was the way it used to be. But I never stopped to listen. I complained loudly that God must be on vacation because He never heard my prayers; He never replied. It was suggested that I was so busy telling God what to do, there was no reason for Him to reply.

Now I get out of bed slowly, get on my knees and pray out loud. That prayer—stripped to its essence: "Thy will be done"—is repeated as I walk the dog, shower, eat breakfast, get dressed. Then I read scripture or meditation, again out loud. I listen. Usually I write thoughts about the reading. I listen some more.

I still pray throughout the days; some days a prayer is necessary every five minutes. But more and more I find that by being still at the beginning of the day, I don't have to be frantic. I don't have to carry around a sense of urgency. I find that God speaks to me over and over again because if I start my day listening, it is easier to go through the day listening. Be still, listen and know that He is God.

**Pray for release from frantic thoughts and actions,
for your life to be filled with the calmness
that allows you to hear God.**

Isaiah 28:14-22; Hebrews 12:18-19, 22-29; Luke 13:22-30

Pam Strickland

58

Proper 17, Sunday Closest to August 31, Year C

Ecclesiasticus 10: (7-11), 12-18. *A long illness baffles the physician.*

Most of our spiritual, physical and emotional illnesses are so long because of our denial that anything is wrong until we are deep into our disease. The alcoholic must reach his or her "bottom" before surrendering to a greater power. The elderly must suffer a fall or a fire before facing the truth about no longer being able to live alone. The workaholic must suffer physical exhaustion or emotional depression before accepting the possibility of a lifestyle change. Our teen-agers often must face a tragic or near-tragic accident before facing immortality.

These character defects are so obvious in other people, but I cannot see them in myself until I too reach bottom. This is why God constantly calls us to community. The denial factor is so great that we cannot see our own illness. We can see it clearly in someone else; and then one day a nerve is hit: "I have been that cruel. I have said those words. I have lost priority in my life. I have forgotten my friends. That addiction is running my life too. I see myself!" I cannot change my friends, but I can change myself. I can be there when my friends hit bottom and remember what it was like when I was there.

My job is to be as alert as possible. If I am so blind to my own defects, I can try to stay open and recognize those character defects which most trouble me in others as probably my own sins as well. Then I must pray that God will change me, for most of these defects are such a part of my being that I have no hope of changing on my own—it is a job for a higher power. An encouraging observation is that sometimes my bottom, the pain and denial I must endure before recognizing my sins is sometimes not as low as in the past.

For today, when you encounter a sin in another that repulses you, ponder if it is in your own heart too. Concentrate on changing yourself rather than your neighbor.

Psalm 112, Hebrews 13:1-8, Luke 14:1, 7-14

Joanna Seibert

Proper 18, Sunday Closest to September 7, Year C

Psalm 1. *So when judgment comes the wicked shall not stand firm, nor shall sinners stand in the assembly of the righteous.*

I have watched an acquaintance of mine in a management position continually use his title to intimidate the staff. This man has enjoyed pulling people close to him to make them confidants while bolstering their egos. Then he begins a systematic breaking down of the subject's spirit and self-worth. Once the subject has become discredited, the manager begins his plays on another, unsuspecting victim.

So many times I have climbed on my white horse to slay this windmill. I have spent many hours listening to those who have suffered from this harsh treatment. I wondered how long one person can justify this behavior. Slowly I learned to believe in the concept of evil.

Then one Sunday the sermon was on God's judgment. By the time I left church, my muscles ached, but my heart was free. God allowed me to release the tension and hatred I felt for this man. He has promised that He will judge, not me. I am not responsible for righting all the wrongs. He gave me peace and His love.

**Pray for those who perpetuate evil
and release their judgment into God's hands.**

Deuteronomy 30:15-20; Philemon 1-20; Luke 14:25-33

Sandra Wheat

Proper 19, Sunday Closest to September 14, Year C

Luke 15:1-10. *"Rejoice with me!" he cries. "I have found my lost sheep."*

It is difficult to avoid seeing the homeless and destitute. Everyone agrees the situation is deplorable that a wealthy nation cannot clothe and feed the needy. But I explain, "I am no social worker. I am not a millionaire to solve these problems." The homeless are not the only people I see with blank, hungry expressions. When I am at work, at church or while shopping, I see lonely eyes every place. These people are fed and warm, but still they have a hunger.

A good friend gives me no advice but gives me the most. While I am talking, she smiles and just says, "Yes, yes." Her presence is an outpouring of God's love and acceptance.

God understands that I can't feed and clothe the homeless. But He gives me an example of what I can do for those who are hungry. The hunger may be for a laugh, a touch, a concern about their lives. The need may be a word of affirmation to remember their self-worth so that they see themselves with as much love as God sees them. I can be His vessel to smile and say, "Yes, yes."

**Pray to be a vessel of God's love and acceptance
for one of His lost sheep.**

Psalm 51:1-18; Exodus 32:1, 7-14; I Timothy 1:12-17

Sandra Wheat

Proper 20, Sunday Closest to September 21, Year C

Luke 16:1-13. *No servant can be the slave of two masters. . . . You cannot serve God and money.*

It is uncomfortable each year at pledge time to review my finances and decide the amount to give to church. I have to think of my entire life and how much time and money I am willing to commit.

My parents did not seem to have this problem. Their church and family were the center of their lives. My brother and I watched Daddy extend credit and make business loans to high-risk people whom even a child would refuse. But the business grew each year. My parents had little education but believed in God and their own hard work.

I attended parties with their retired friends. I saw the eagerness of these friends to share a joke or moment of sadness with them. They had time to share a project or cook a meal when needed. Only when my brother and I were much older did we realize that we should not have been concerned for our parents' lack of business acumen. Without thinking of laying up worldly treasures, these two loving stewards had become very rich.

Pray for a generous heart. Pray that stewardship of gifts is an opportunity, not an obligation.

Psalm 138; Amos 8:4-7, (8-12); I Timothy 2:1-8

Sandra Wheat

Proper 21, Sunday Closest to September 28, Year C

Luke 16:19-31. *The poor man died and was carried away by the angels.*

Quiet miracles? Loud miracles? What will it take for us to believe? As I reflect on my own life, there are times when I have been more anxious to know *about* rather than to *know* God. As the wife of a priest, I thought somehow that it was my duty and responsibility to look the part of the devoted Christian, even though I did not always feel the part. To me, my Christian life sometimes seemed a facade. Then as only God can in His gentle way, He took my thought and action faith-threads and began to unravel them and then ravel them around the strong threads of His Word.

One such instance was at the time of the death of my mother-in-law, Kathryn. My husband and his sister sat quietly with their mother as she took and held her last breath. A mother's son gave her last rites through his own tears, trying to soothe his sister's grief, wanting to commit his mother to God, needing to be comforted at his new loss. Through their grief, I saw the strong tapestry of their faith, and the tapestry of my faith was strengthened—peaceful assurance in the midst of hot, wet tears and hard grief. It was like Lazarus coming to cool hot tongues in flames of agony; but in this case, it was not Lazarus but Jesus who came; and Jesus was not prohibited or prevented from coming to them.

In torment, a rich man protested that Moses was not enough for his brothers; it would take someone rising from the dead for them to believe. We do, indeed, have the One before us who has risen from the dead. Jesus, the risen Lord, meets us in Sacrament, in the Word, in righteous need, and when two or three gather in His name. In a hospital room with a dying woman and mother, son and daughter were there in His name, and He was there. "I am the resurrection and the life. She who believes in me though she die shall not die forever."

Lord, you were there. What more will it take for us to believe?
Lord, we do believe! Help us in our unbelief!

Psalm 146; Amos 6:1-7; I Timothy 6:11-19

Suzanne Pyron

Proper 22, Sunday Closest to October 5, Year C

Luke 17:5-10. *If you had faith the size of a mustard seed....*

A resolution for me at the beginning of this new year is to watch for and expect some miracle each day.

On the morning of Mike's funeral, as I was working with a dental patient, my mind drifted to the lessons I would read at the burial office. I remembered sitting with Mike's parents as they selected the lessons and hymns for the service, and I remembered silently crying as their loss settled on me. I remembered silently asking God to help me read the passages of scripture at Mike's funeral with a conviction and gentleness that would communicate their meaning.

While working with my patient, suddenly I saw a vivid rainbow flash almost imperceptibly. This had never happened before in my many years of practice. A rainbow, sign of another promise of God long ago and sign of promise to me in that dental office. In that moment, I knew that Michael had received Him of whom we can only dream and imagine. God's promise was sure, and in a moment my faith was rainbow clearer.

How much faith do we need? The disciples of Jesus asked Him to give them more faith. He said that they had enough and that even a small amount of their faith could command mulberry trees to be uprooted and planted into the sea. In rainbow days, I found faith; and the receiving of a rainbow miracle sign did for me far greater things than uprooting and replanting trees.

Psalm 37:1-18; Habakkuk 1:1-6, (7-11), 12-13, 2:1-4; II Timothy 1:(1-5), 6-14

Suzanne Pyron

Proper 23, Sunday Closest to October 12, Year C

Ruth 1:(1-7), 8-19a. *And Ruth said, "Entreat me not to leave thee, or return from following after thee; for whither thou goest, I will go; and where thou lodgest, I will lodge; thy people shall be my people, and thy God my God."*

I have always thought these to be some of the most beautiful verses in the Bible, the ultimate expression of loyalty. I consider myself lucky to be, like Ruth, a woman with a mother-in-law that I can follow. I am not a widow who has had to follow her to a strange land, but I can follow my mother-in-law's example. Our religions are not the same—she is a Christian Scientist—but we certainly worship the same God; and by knowing her, I am less prone to make those trite judgments we sometimes make toward those in other religions.

The main thing she has taught me is not to try to unduly influence others toward my point of view. (I have not finished learning this lesson.) This is actually a part of her religion—that when we try to manipulate someone toward an action or point of view, we are interfering with their free will and may actually be interfering with God's intervention and influence. I feel that God sends specific people into our lives to help us find our way to Him. They may be in our families or churches or in another religion entirely. Whatever our relationship, the most important one is that of fellow travelers. As "The Servant Song"* so beautifully expresses, "We are pilgrims on a journey, we are travelers on the road, we are here to help each other, walk the mile and bear the load."

**Thank God for the people who have helped lead you
in your journey. Thank them too.**

Psalm 113; II Timothy 2:(3-7), 8-15; Luke 17:11-19

Diane Plunkett

*Cry Hosanna, by Richard Gillard, p. 117

Proper 24, Sunday Closest to October 19, Year C

Psalm 121. *I will lift up mine eyes unto the hills, from whence cometh my help, my help cometh from the Lord, which made heaven and earth.*

These verses have so much more meaning for me since last winter when I saw the Rocky Mountains for the first time. One doesn't see these mountains with the eyes alone but experiences them, is enveloped by them and blessed by the nearness of their Maker. It is to the things of God in this world that we look for signs of His presence. We may be in awe of great art, wonderful woman- or man-made beauty, but surely nothing we make can compare with what God creates.

I can't imagine anyone ever writing, "I will lift mine eyes unto the skyscraper, from whence cometh my help." But we do this in our lives by looking everywhere for the answers to our problems but to the source of all wholeness and the giver of all good things.

I have wondered if people who live beneath the mountains eventually take them for granted and forget to "lift up their eyes" just as we often are too busy or distracted to feel God's nearness in our daily lives.

**Lord, open our eyes and hearts to the beauty, majesty
and indescribable goodness of your presence in our world.**

Genesis 32:3-8, 22-30; II Timothy 3:14-4:5; Luke 18:1-8a

Diane Plunkett

Proper 25, Sunday Closest to October 26, Year C

Jeremiah 14. *Yet you, oh Lord, are in the midst of us, and we are called by your name. . . . We look for peace, but there is no good; for a time of healing, but there is terror instead.*

Contrasts? Inconsistencies? Contradictions?—All within one chapter of Jeremiah.

My neighbor's elderly parents were involved in a terrible car accident and were in critical condition for weeks. Their daughter said, "The Lord was with them." I asked myself, "Why then did this awful thing happen?"

In our city, street gangs proliferate. Rivals are continuously at war as the year's murder rate soars past all records. For some, death is a gracious end to hunger, pain and suffering. Yet still we contend that "You, oh Lord, are in the midst of us."

A lady I know has a "hat ministry." She regularly fills her car with hats, socks and gloves, which she distributes to anyone in need of her gifts. Her neighborhood, by contrast, is the same one that produces local gangsters. Surely she represents God in our midst. The grateful daughter's perspective, when surrounded by the terror of her parents' wreck, does too.

What does Jeremiah say to us from so many centuries ago? He struggled with paradox just as we do.

Why are we surrounded with so many problems if God is really with us? Do we bring them on ourselves by our gross iniquities? Is God's presence real or just a coping device? Each day we wrest with the "terror" of our daily lives and our faith that the Lord is "in our midst."

Our challenge is to move beyond and through the troubles into the Lord's presence. Perhaps it is a matter of our own perspective.

**This week try to see instances of God "in the midst of us,"
especially in situations of terror and strife. Help us Lord,
to view the paradoxes of this life with understanding,
based in the knowledge of your love,
so that our faith may be strengthened
and not diminished. Amen.**

Psalm 84; II Timothy 4:6-8, 16-18; Luke 18:9-14

Jacque Alexander

All Saints' Day, November 1, Year C

Revelation 7:2-4, 9-17. *. . . They are before the throne of God, and worship Him day and night within His temple, and the one who is seated on the throne will shelter them.*

My oldest child turns 16 today. So many motherly thoughts run through my head as he begins the transition from childhood to adulthood. For these years, I have done all in my power to give him what I could to help form a solid Christian character and protect him as best I could from any evils that the world put in his way. Sometimes I was more successful than others.

Now I have to be more intentional about letting go. He can drive alone and does not need me in the way he did before. Now is the time for both him and me to remember and trust that God is the one who will shelter him. Reread the passage from Revelation. As I learn to give up my son to adulthood, I give him also to join the great multitudes of saints who are surrounding God in heaven. In my son's short life, he has already faced ordeals and certainly will face many more in the future. My assurance is that God and these, robed in white, will be with him in his future journey.

It is hard for a mother to let go. It is hard to admit that my child can and must make it on his own. He must learn things the hard way and be allowed to fail. Yet God has given us the assurance that no matter what happens here in this life, if we trust in Him, we will hunger no more, thirst no more and not be victim to the scorching heat.

For years I have wiped away the tears in my child's eyes. He will be gone from me soon, and I hope that he will depend on God's love to do the same. And I know that other living saints will be there for him. God does not expect us to make the journey alone but provides us with multitudes of holy persons who will touch our lives if we are open to receive them.

Pray for all persons going through life's transitions.
Pray that someone will be there for them and that
they will be open to accept help, love
and encouragement on their journey.

Psalm 149; Ecclesiasticus 2:1-11; Matthew 5:1-12

Jo Ann Barker

Proper 26, Sunday Closest to November 2, Year C

Luke 19:1-10. *For the Son of Man came to seek out and to save the lost.*

Each time I read the story of Zacchaeus, the childhood song, "Zacchaeus was a wee little man, a wee little man was he . . ." runs through my head.

Zacchaeus was the town scoundrel—a crooked tax collector who became rich by cheating his fellow man. Surely he was held in low esteem. The song's description of Zacchaeus as a "wee little man" probably reflected his personality as much as his stature.

So why, of all people, did Jesus choose Zacchaeus to visit? Couldn't the Lord's advance men, the disciples, have known about Zacchaeus and found a more appropriate host for the King of Kings? Surely the town had priests, doctors or people of great faith, who would have been richly rewarded by the Lord's visit. It would have reinforced their good examples to the common people.

Yet Jesus not only sought out Zacchaeus, but chose him to visit and "brought salvation to his house." Luke's story tells us that Zacchaeus repented and vowed to change his ways. He promised to give half of his possessions to the poor and to return all the money he had stolen from his neighbors fourfold.

The message here, while obvious, bears repeating. Lives can be dramatically changed. Jesus came to find and save the sinners (which incidentally includes us all), and none is too lowly for Him and redemption. Alleluia!

Pay attention to the judgments you pronounce on others. The next time you are tempted to sneer to yourself concerning someone else's "shortcomings" or if you personally feel unlovable or unimportant, remember the story of Zacchaeus. Help us, oh Lord, to see your divine image in each person we encounter. Help us to remember how important we are to you. Amen.

Psalm 32; Isaiah 1:10-20; II Thessalonians 1:1-5, (6-10), 11-12

Jacque Alexander

Proper 27, Sunday Closest to November 9, Year C

II Thessalonians 2:13-3:5. *So then (sisters) stand firm and hold to the teachings we passed on to you, whether by word of mouth or by letter.*

Paul's instructions here leave no doubt as to his expectation. Standing firm is easy, as is holding to the teachings . . . as long as we are not challenged! Friends tell me that by holding firm they "grow deeper roots." For me it is always a tentative undertaking because I'm easily swayed by ideas, thoughts, writings and people.

It was always my idea that I should bend so as not to break. But I'm learning to have more self-confidence in the teachings—and I'm learning to find a stronger foundation.

**Thank God for family and friends
who share Christian love and support.**

Psalm 17; Job 19:23-27a; Luke 20:27, (28-33), 34-38

Virginia Kutait

Proper 28, Sunday Closest to November 16, Year C

Psalm 98. *Make a joyful noise unto the Lord all the earth: make a loud noise and rejoice and sing praise.*

After a life-threatening illness to a family member, we left the hospital to return to our room to rest. We were quiet and sad-faced in spite of the fact that all had gone well. The enthusiasm we should have been feeling was subdued.

The elevator operator was an elderly man. He had been there many years, had seen us before and knew of our plight.

"How did the surgery go?" he asked.

"Just great," we replied.

"Well then," he answered, "you must act happy; you must sing and praise the Lord because that's what He wants you to do."

We looked at each other in amazement, began laughing and acknowledged our great fortune in the healing of our loved one!

**Today thank God for someone who has reminded you
of what God wants you to do.**

Malachi 3:13-4:2a, 5-6; Luke 21:5-19

Virginia Kutait

Proper 29, Sunday Closest to November 23, Year C

Colossians 1:11-20. *He has rescued us from the power of darkness and transferred us into the kingdom of the His beloved Son, in whom we have redemption, the forgiveness of sins.*

What assurance there is in Paul's statement to the faithful in Christ in Colossae! Paul continues by telling the Colossians that he prays each day "that you may live a life worthy of the Lord . . . bearing fruit in every good work . . . growing in the knowledge of God."

To be rescued from darkness is no small thing. It is the object of this journey we call life. When we bear good fruit and grow in knowledge, we become better related people, to God, to others and to ourselves.

Redemption and forgiveness are offered as spiritual gifts free for the taking.

It is a simple challenge but a complex undertaking. Many times we find it impossible to achieve Paul's "one-mindness," to pray with his intensity, thankfulness and clarity. Because it is so easy to become distracted, we lose the focus of a life worthy of the Lord and forget that the advantage of living is not measured by length, but by use!

**Today let us use our lives for the Glory of God
and pray for the fruits of faith, love and hope.**

Jeremiah 23:1-6; Luke 23:35-43; Luke 19:29-38; Psalm 46

Virginia Kutait

YEAR A
1995-1996

PURIFY OUR CONSCIENCE ALMIGHTY GOD BY YOUR DAILY VISITATION, THAT YOUR SON JESUS CHRIST

AT HIS COMING MAY FIND IN US A MANSION PREPARED

FOR HIMSELF; WHO LIVES AND REIGNS WITH YOU IN THE UNITY OF THE HOLY SPIRIT, ONE GOD —

Advent 1, Year A

Psalm 122. *Our feet are standing within your gates O Jerusalem. . . .*
Pray for the peace of Jerusalem.

There is an ancient and beautiful word of praise, *majeed*, whose meaning connotes "the splendor of God made visible." Such are our associations with Jerusalem, along with the yearning for unity, blessing, peace. We yearn for these as we yearn for the Savior.

Jerusalem . . . On the day before Easter, a lady from our city walked the stations of the cross there four days after I had undergone critical surgery. What a gift.

How can we bring Jerusalem within? "Be ready . . ." to see the splendor daily as we sometimes do with people of presence or places of wonder. We no longer assume an orderly world or an orderly life. But we can stand in that holy spaciousness and trust the unfolding of divine order in our lives.

O come, O come, Emmanuel. Thanks be to God.

Isaiah 2:1-5; Romans 13:8-14, Matthew 24:37-44

Dodi Walton Horne

Isaiah 11:1-10. *A shoot shall come out from the stump of Jesse, and a branch shall grow out of his roots.*

Pointing out work I wanted done in my yard last spring, I said to the gardener, "And will you please cut that sprout out of the ivy bed?" The gardener looked at me in dismay as he answered, "Oh, Ma'am, I never like to cut down a dogwood tree; and that's a fine, healthy, young dogwood."

My mind raced immediately to the passage in Isaiah: "A shoot shall come out from the stump of Jesse, and a branch shall grow out from his roots."

A pink dogwood I had planted with loving care and high hopes had died a couple of years earlier. Seeing no hope for life and blossoms, I had the tree cut down. Now a fine, young tree has grown up from its roots! Its identity was hidden from me—but recognized and appreciated by the gardener.

How like the story of Jesus! A shoot from the branch of Jesse! Unrecognized by so many—this branch from Jesse's roots was cut down with no gardener to recognize him!

But Jesus rose again in full splendor—healthy, in full leaf, in full power, ready and eager to bring each of us to live with Him in His kingdom!

**Pray that we may recognize and value the face of Jesus
in the unlikely faces around us.**

Psalm 72; Romans 15:4-13; Matthew 3:1-12

Nyna Keeton

Advent 3, Year A

Psalm 146. *God will reign for all time.*
Isaiah 35:1-10. *The blind will see, the deaf hear, the lame leap and dance, those unable to speak will shout for joy.*
James 5:7-10. *Remember the prophets and their patient endurance under suffering.*
Matthew 11:2-11. *John sent word by His disciples asking, "Are you he who is to come or shall we look for another?"*

The Jews took seriously the commandment to make no graven images and would therefore never draw a picture of God or describe God in physical terms, such as "an old man with blue eyes and a long, white beard who lived in the clouds." Instead, if you asked what God was like, you would get what Psalm 146 uses as a description: God keeps His promises, judges in favor of the oppressed, gives food to the hungry (spiritual food to the spiritually hungry too), sets prisoners free, gives sight to the blind, lifts those who have fallen, protects strangers, widows and orphans, loves His righteous people.

Jesus replied to the disciples of John with the reminder to him of the quote from Isaiah. Alas, John did not get to live to see the crucifixion and resurrection and to find how deep, high and broad is the love of God. Should a Messiah be a servant?

**Remember in your prayers this day those known to you
who do not know the Lord Jesus and whose lives seem
desperate and empty. Hold them up to the life
and light which came into the world.**

Anne Fulk

Matthew 1:18-25. *Her husband Joseph, being a righteous man and unwilling to expose her to public disgrace, planned to dismiss her quietly . . . an angel of the Lord appeared to him in a dream and said, "Joseph . . . do not be afraid to take Mary as your wife, for the child conceived in her is from the Holy Spirit."*

This week's gospel shows Joseph's conflict between hiding his secret shame (marriage to a pregnant woman) and God's call to be faithful to God's wish. He is asked to take a risk and help fulfill the prophecy that Emmanuel—God Is with Us—is to be born.

How often, when ashamed or overwhelmed with a pregnant teen-ager, a child or sibling with AIDS, failed business, lost expectations of a "normal" family life—how often do we isolate from others, turn inward, feel punished or victimized?

Yet the hope in this reading is that God uses every experience, every relationship in our lives, to join together in the birth-rebirth story. We are called to trust God's knowing, His wisdom, His will not ours, to learn the truth: God is with us.

> **This week read Hymn 702, "Lord, Thou hast searched me,"**
> **(*The Hymnal*, 1982). Look at secrets you carry.**
> **What decisions do you make to "save face, be proper,**
> **not show what's really happening in your life"?**
> **Make a list. Read this list during your Christmas**
> **confession. Take Eucharist on Christmas Eve**
> **knowing Emmanuel—God Is with Us—is here.**
> **Alleluia!**

Psalm 24; Isaiah 7:10-17; Romans 1:1-7

Pan Adams

Christmas Day, Year A

Luke 2:1-14, (15-20). *But Mary treasured all these words and pondered them in her heart.*

How can a story so familiar make any difference, I ponder. How can it really make a meaningful impact in the life I live . . . or the life within me?

Every year the world begins to prepare earlier and earlier for Christmas. Every year I begin planning later and later. This year our family decided to give gifts only to our little children. Without the pressure of finding something really perfect for each member of my family, the week before Christmas came suddenly like a thief in the night. (It took me three full days to decorate one tree and one mantle and put a bow on some greenery outside my door). This year we "pot-lucked" the family Christmas Eve dinner, each bringing just what we wanted to cook or had time to make. The Christmas Eve service at our church was deeply holy with voices, music, flowers, candles, children sleepily propped against bosoms warm and safe.

Family: This is the natal womb out of which streams forth the body and blood of God silently, in stillness, small and sweet. Family ritual: Around my dining table, we receive food prepared by each of us; around the altar, we receive bread and wine prepared by each of us.

The moment of midnight comes softly. We slip into the nativity of our Lord Jesus Christ. He is born in us so that we may be born in Him.

> **In what ways do I experience the celebration**
> **of the nativity of Jesus Christ's impact on:**
> **My family? individually and as a whole;**
> **My church? as individuals, clergy, friends, family;**
> **The world? the poor, the rich; peace, governments;**
> **the gift of the earth; My life as a Christian?**

Psalm 96; Isaiah 9:2-4, 6-7; Titus 2:11-14

Merry Helen Hedges

Psalm 147. *He gives to the beasts their food, and to the young ravens when they cry.*

I have just spent three weeks observing God's creation and provision of food for that creation. I was visiting my son who is in the Peace Corps in Swaziland, Africa. We spent several days in Botswana and Zimbabwe, where we went on numerous "game drives." The very first one provided us with a view of a lioness who had killed a giraffe and was enjoying a rest after the kill and a meal of giraffe leg. The next morning six more lions joined the lioness for two days of feasting. Waiting patiently in nearby trees and bush were the vultures and hyenas. Their turn would come later.

The way of nature seems cruel and arbitrary, and I was rather frightened sitting in the open vehicle that close to lions. This psalm reminded me that God has created the lion, the giraffe and me. God has provided for all of us. God knows our names, needs and desires. God knows our worries, fears and hopes.

> **Is there something about which you are concerned,**
> **something you deeply need or desire? Place that concern**
> **in God's hands and watch the solution unfold**
> **(It may not be what you want.)**
> **Be open to what happens.**
> **God's provision is often a surprise beyond**
> **our imagining or deserving.**

Isaiah 61:10-62:3; Galatians 3:23-25, 4:4-7; John 1:1-18

Sandy Finkbeiner

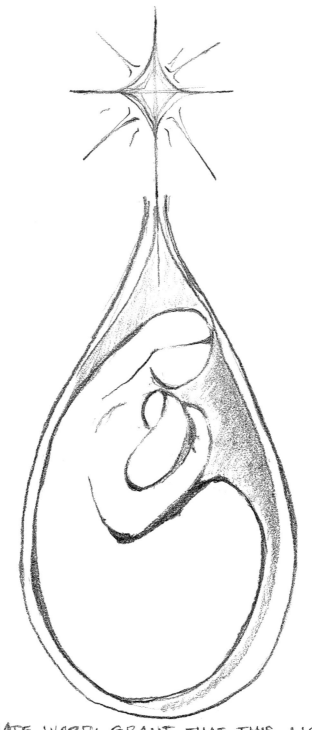

ALMIGHTY GOD, YOU HAVE POURED UPON US THE NEW LIGHT OF YOUR

ENKINDLED IN OUR HEARTS, MAY SHINE FORTH IN OUR LIVES. AMEN.

INCARNATE WORD: GRANT THAT THIS LIGHT,

Epiphany, Year A

Isaiah 60:1-6, 9. *Arise, shine; for your light has come.*

Epiphany, the revelation, the manifestation of Christ to the gentiles—us, you and me. Christ is indeed manifested to me almost sensuously at Epiphany. It first happened in the mid-'50s, when I attended my first Episcopal service at the Epiphany Feast of Lights in a small Virginia church with a boyfriend and his family. I still remember so many details. I needed to wear a hat. I ended up with a small, black chapel veil. I was overpowered by the first encounter with the liturgy, candlelight and unfamiliar haunting, mystic melodies. As we walked out of the small-town church on that bitter, cold January night, carrying our candles, we were surprised by the winter's first unexpected snow.

I knew that night that God spoke most clearly to me through the Episcopal church. It was ten years later before I answered that call, this time offered by the dean of the cathedral in Memphis. His acceptance of me in my humanness, often with great joy and humor, gave me a hint that God might do the same. The Epiphany Feast of Lights was an important event at the Memphis cathedral, with the gospel read by the Greek orthodox priest and a choral procession of the costumed wise men bearing great gifts. The cathedral was always packed. The choir and candlelight recessional out of the church into the dark night also was breathtaking.

I always left feeling empowered to "think about" carrying my light into the world. I can still see other anxious faces walking out ahead of me, those people tightly gripping their small candles. "What will we encounter next in the night?"

I also remember the great light generated by all of us together. I delight that God chooses to speak through so many sensual sights, sounds and smells—music, smoke, costumes, candlelight, snowflakes, incense, languages now foreign to us.

**Tonight attend a Feast of Lights service. If you cannot,
go outside, light your candle, read Isaiah 60:1-6,
and feel, smell, hear and see God calling you by name
in the beauty of this winter night.**

Psalm 72; Ephesians 3:1-12; Matthew 2:1-12

Joanna Seibert

Epiphany 1, Year A

Isaiah 42:1-9. *I have put my spirit upon him; He will bring forth justice to the nations.*

To look at my house, you can't tell Christmas was in full swing two or three weeks ago. All the decorations have been stored for next year, the music put away and the tree hauled off.

What about the inner signs? Is there any evidence that God was born as a little baby—as the hymn says, "God made manifest in man?" (*The Hymnal*, 1982, No. 135.) Will I also stash away until next Christmas my astonishment that God became human?

Isaiah reminds us that God made a commitment to us and that Jesus is part of that covenant. It is through the fusion of God and human that He will "open the eyes that are blind" and free prisoners from darkness.

In this new year's world, though, I see injustice, blindness and captivity. In fact, it's impossible to escape the cruelty, oppression, injustice and misery of our shrinking world. Where *is* that God-Human now?

Peter answers my questions by reminding me of Jesus' work: "He went about doing good and healing all who were oppressed by the devil, for God was with him." There is oppression, cruelty and injustice—now as when Jesus lived. But the good news is God loves me and it's with *my* life that goodness and healing can come into the world. And best of all, I'm not the source; I'm the vehicle. Just as God empowered Jesus with the Holy Spirit, so I am empowered.

When I return to school next week, I have the opportunity to put the Christmas experience to work. First, I must open my eyes to my blindness to my inner darkness and my actions toward others. Second, I must identify where I'm held captive from life by that feeling of helplessness that holds me back. And third, with God's help, I can "bring from the prison those who sit in darkness." The key word here is *sit*. There certainly is a time to be still, but when I imprison myself in inaction when a response is being called for, I shut myself off from God's light.

The celebration of Christmas is finished. It has led us into an Epiphany. It is a time to "see, the former things have come to pass, and new things I now declare."

Psalm 89:1-29; Acts 10:34-38; Matthew 3:13-17

Deb Meisch

Epiphany 2, Year A

John 1:29-41.

I just don't pay attention when I should. I can't remember names; and worse than that, sometimes I don't remember people that I've met several times. Many times I see someone whom I'm accustomed to seeing in a particular place and associate the person with that place; but when I see this person in a different place, my mind goes blank. I have no idea who this person is or from where I know him or her.

I have the same problem many times in recognizing Christ. My mind is so preoccupied with other concerns that I have little or no room for spiritual awareness. I, of course, look for Him in church; but during the week when I see Him, sometimes I don't recognize Him because I'm not looking. It's hard to recognize someone I don't expect.

At other times, I look very hard for Christ, and I can't find Him because I don't know how He looks. I might be standing in His presence and not know it. I have a great deal of work to do in training my eyes and heart to see Christ in day-to-day events and in ordinary people. But through the grace of God, no matter how many times I fail to recognize Christ, He will continue to be in my presence and help me to know that He is standing with me.

"Whenever you fed the hungry, you fed me; whenever you clothed the naked, you clothed me; whenever you cared for the sick, you cared for me."

Pray that Christ will help us be more aware of
His presence in everyday life and that others
will recognize Christ in our lives.

Psalm 40:1-10; Isaiah 49:1-7; I Corinthians 1:1-9

Sammye Dewoody

Epiphany 3, Year A

Psalm 139:1-17. *O Lord, you know it completely.*

For most of my adult life, I have struggled with the abortion issue and, I must confess, have been a pro-choice advocate for the majority of that time. I could not support the belief that a woman must have the government's permission to seek a safe, legal medical procedure to end an unplanned pregnancy, nor did I believe that physicians should risk the loss of their profession in an attempt to provide that service. In some cases, the decision to have a baby (forced or voluntary) could jeopardize careers, marriages or health. That decision could sever families, create financial hardships and even cause emotional distress to the point of suicide.

A paradox always existed in my mind when conservative, pro-life proponents added exceptions to their convictions, as in the case of rape or incest. If, as these people believed, abortion was indeed murder, why would it not be the same for a child who was conceived under any circumstances?

Today's scripture spoke a new message to me. "Thine eyes have seen my unformed substance. . . . The days that were ordained for me, when as yet there was not one of them" (verse 16). Does this mean that each and every one of us was planned long before our parents even knew us? Is each one of us here for a purpose—God's purpose?

For those who have to make this decision, Christ is there. It is not my place nor anyone else's to condemn or judge those who make these personal decisions, but now it is my responsibility to stand up for new insights while providing love and support to those who do not agree with me.

**Pray for those who face difficult decisions
and help them to realize "How wonderful are your works."**

Amos 3:1-8; I Corinthians 1:10-17; Matthew 4:12-23

Scottie Healy

Epiphany 4, Year A

Matthew 5:1-12. *Blessed are those of a gentle spirit, they shall have the earth for their possession.*

The more familiar translation of this beatitude is: "Blessed are the meek, for they shall inherit the earth." But I like the New English Version because I have known people blessed with a gentle spirit—living, breathing saints, gentlemen and gentlewomen. Unfortunately *meek* has a more "wimpish" connotation for me.

In everyday language, this beatitude is saying to me: Blessed are those who don't need to run the show, to get the biggest piece of the pie, throw their weight around and prove how great they are.

And finally, blessed are those who don't try to control others—associates, family, friends. When I give up trying to control, it doesn't mean I'll inherit more of the things of this earth. I won't be wealthier, more popular, more powerful. But I may earn the respect of my associates, thanks and love of my family and gratitude and trust of my friends. And I can inherit the peace of mind that comes from knowing the situation is in God's hands.

Bishop John Coburn, the retired Bishop of Massachusetts, wrote in *The Hope of Glory*: "When Jesus zaps you . . . you have a sense that you no longer have to be in charge of yourself. God is. When this happens, your love of others turns from possessing them to affirming them, helping them become renewed, more whole. . . ."

**This week try not to run the show.
Pray for a gentle spirit.**

Psalm 37:1-18; Micah 6:1-8; I Corinthians 1:26-31

Betty Rowland

Epiphany 5, Year A

Psalm 27. *I believe I shall see the goodness of the Lord in the land of the living.*

Epiphany is the time when we proclaim the light, tell of the goodness of God, share our joy, tell of our "high places" and let our own light shine.

How can this happen? Won't our friends and co-workers think we're mad if we talk about joy and goodness when television and newspapers are proclaiming daily that violence, crime, rape, abuse, corruption, addiction and AIDS are increasing?

The lessons for Epiphany 5 address this dilemma. The psalmist St. Paul and prophet Habakkuk also were surrounded by pestilence and plague. Yet these readings tell us they rejoiced, saw beauty, felt sheltered, demonstrated power and spirit. They were "the salt of the earth" in their time.

How this happens is a secret—a spiritual secret. St. Paul calls it "the secret and hidden wisdom of God," a "demonstration of the Spirit." We can't explain it, but we too know that it happens. In the midst of a crisis, we feel hope. In the midst of an argument, we begin to laugh. When faced with uncertainty, we somehow know things will work out. In the face of fatal illness, we have a moment of peace or a gut feeling of joy. We experience a coincidence that seems like a miracle. When we claim and proclaim those moments of grace, we are being the light for today's world. When we share them with others, we are prophets and psalmists.

Writing of our experiences, insights and wisdom in this book of meditation is a way of being the salt of the earth for our time, of imparting the secret wisdom of God. Reading these meditations, thinking about them and discussing them with others are also ways to claim our "glorification." So let's be it and claim it.

**This week I will not only admit my fears and frustrations,
I will watch for my "high places." I shall see the goodness in the
land of the living, and I will share my experience
with at least one other person. This is my light,
and I will let it shine.**

Habakkuk 3:2-6, 17-19; I Corinthians 2:1-11; Matthew 5:13-20

Trudy James

Epiphany 6, Year A

Psalm 119:1-16. *With my whole heart I seek you.*

All the lessons and the psalm for this Sunday speak to me of freedom, consistency and the importance of my inner attitudes.

In the back of my mind somewhere, I tell myself, it is appropriate to, and that some day I will, wait in prayer until I know what is God's will for me in any given situation and that only then will I act on that knowledge.

But these lessons teach me that the issue is not so much what I do but how I do it: how I relate to people and whether or not I see all of them—each one—as valued and precious to God; whether or not I treat each one with the same respect and love as I would if I truly believed they were all I would ever see of God—certainly in this world; whether or not I am willing to give up control of these situations, of my involvement in them and of the outcome, shifting the focus from Wednesday's agenda and next month's committee commitment to the way I participate and how participation affects the other aspects of my life.

And that is where I must let God in. That is where I must give God control over the priorities of my life and the way I carry them out. Giving up that control for me is the hard thing to do.

**Pray for clarity in your own decision-making
and for the grace to give up to God control
of your priorities and attitudes.**

Ecclesiasticus 15:11-20; I Corinthians 3:1-9; Matthew 5:21-24, 27-30, 33-37

Madge Brown

Matthew 5:38-48. *Be ye therefore perfect, even as your Father which is in heaven is perfect.*

It is beyond coincidence that this problematic passage would be assigned to me for a meditation. All my life I have striven for perfection. As a small child, I recall struggling to do my homework perfectly, staying up until all hours to check and recheck, write and rewrite. In adulthood, I was forced to take a hard look at the condition I was in because of my compulsion to be perfect. Only then did I begin to discern the difference between my definition of perfection and God's definition.

When my daughter completed the first grade, her teacher and principal recommended that she skip the second grade. She was academically gifted, and they suggested that we evaluate her social maturity. During the test, the counselor asked her what she would change if she could change one thing about herself. With great conviction, she replied, "Oh, I wouldn't change anything. I'm perfect just the way I am." This youngster realized that God had created her to be herself and that was perfection.

I, on the other hand, spent several decades trying to convince God and myself that *perfection* meant "free from sin." Recently a wise colleague admonished me to strive for progress, for excellence, not perfection. It is my constant battle.

Ask for guidance to do good and be perfect.
Pray you will be the perfect person God created you to be.

Psalm 71; Leviticus 19:1-2, 9-18; I Corinthians 3:10-11, 16-23

Dean McMillin

Ash Wednesday, Year A

Psalm 103. *God remembers that we are but dust.*

On Ash Wednesday, the priest marks us with the sign of the cross with ashes on our foreheads and says, "Remember that you are but dust, and to dust you shall return."

This is a time to remember our mortality; it is a time to remember we do not live forever. It is a time to remember that we are mortal, we are frail, we are vulnerable.

It is in living into that frailness and vulnerability, in letting our egos be at rest, that we can know more fully that God is with us and in us. Regrettably we often try to avoid, even deny at times, those feelings of frailness, vulnerability and mortality. And they can be uncomfortable and scary.

But if we take that step into our fear and our pain, rather than running from it, we know God's presence in us and around us.

And the ashes on our foreheads become our friend, a friend that we welcome and embrace, and we know God in a more intimate way.

Ashes to ashes, and dust to dust.
Thanks be to God.

Joel 2:1-2, 12-17; II Corinthians 5:20b-6:10; Matthew 6:1-6, 16-21

Peggy Hays

Romans 5:12-19, (20-21). Therefore just as sin entered the world through one man, and death came through sin, and so death spread to all because all have sinned.

Cleaning out my attic storeroom is a chore I put off until the urge to clean comes over me. The spring cleaning bug bit me as I was trying to prepare our house to sell. The things I have stored have familiar places in my heart. Perhaps I will need them some day, even if I haven't used them for two years at least. To be honest, even if I could wear some of the old clothes, they would be out of style. Their familiarity seems to be comforting. I have moved ahead of the usefulness of these things, yet I continue to cling. It's time now to let them die.

As Christ died for us, He calls each one of us to experience death in preparation for our shared resurrection. The season of Lent is a perfect time to examine our sins and prepare for their death in us. Making a conscious decision to let the ungodly parts of us die is a first step. Yet this death is change, and change is difficult because of our reluctance to alter familiar surroundings and habits for an uncertain future. It seems to be human nature to fear the unknown. It is comforting to be reminded again and again that, as in verse 17, through Christ's death on the cross, we have been given the gift of righteousness and grace. We are free to let our sins die.

**Dear Lord, allow me to acknowledge my faults
and let them die so I may see and accept your
promises in the new light of dawn.**

Psalm 51; Genesis 2:4b-9, 15-17, 25-3:7; Matthew 4:1-11

Jenny Jackson

Lent 2, Year A

Romans 4:1-5, (6-12), 13-17. *For the promise to Abraham, that he should inherit the world, did not come from observing the Law but through the righteousness of faith.*

I remember driving down Cantrell Road one bright afternoon and having what for me was a revelation—a thought out of the blue that I had never considered before but that made clear and perfect sense. God is not keeping a list of who sleeps with whom or which laws each of us is breaking daily. That's not the point with Him. What He wants us to know is that the laws of human nature exist, just as natural laws, such as the law of gravity exist; and if we break them, there will be pain and consequences.

We get in trouble when we prefer our way to God's and put ourselves in the center, where only God belongs. Our all-encompassing self-centeredness is the attitude that can destroy us and our relationship with God, not the fact that He is keeping a list of our shortcomings and expects us to pay. He has promised us that He has already paid for those Himself and has wiped our ledger clean.

So what then is our task? Maybe it is to become complete, to become all that He has created us to be. This won't happen all at once or to the faint of heart or to those who give up easily. It is a process, and that process, that path to wholeness, is not goodness. It is stumbling and getting up again, facing what we are doing that is not working, and facing that we can't fix it alone. Then we can look beyond our own egos to God and let Him possess our being and become our center.

We have so many weaknesses and faults, and yet we have one wonderful quality: We can change. How important it is that we remain open to change, for that is where growth lies! God has laid out before each of us a path of eternal growth. Keeping the rules 100 percent won't help you know the path; but love of and delight in God will, compassion and love for your neighbor will, and compassion and love for yourself will.

List three things about you worth keeping.
List three things about you worth changing and begin.

Psalm 33:12-22; Genesis 12:1-8; John 3:1-17

Phyllis Raney

John 4:5-26, (27-38), 39-42. *The water that I will give will become in them a spring of water gushing up to eternal life.*

The woman at the well is one of the most remarkable stories in the Bible. What makes this woman so remarkable is that she is a cynical, defeated, ostracized person who, for some reason, believes what Jesus promises her about life. Jesus talked about it all the time: "The water that I will give will become in them a spring of water gushing up to eternal life."

Is Jesus talking about life after death, or is He talking about now? I keep a quotation from Carl Sandburg in my kitchen window. It says: "I am an idealist. I don't know where I am going, but I am on my way." God's life is all around and within us—the air we breathe, blood we bleed, faces we see, sounds we hear, food we cook, wine we drink, flesh we touch, souls we cherish—it is all life. If we would follow Jesus, we must reach out and touch life, for we will touch Jesus. We must take life in our arms and hold it to our breast, and we will embrace the heart of Christ. It is life, Jesus' gift to us. Share it with Him.

Today if you want it, affirmatively say, "I want to live your abundant life, Jesus, my Lord. Thank you. Amen." The prayer of life. Live it.

Psalm 95; Exodus 17:1-7; Romans 5:1-11

Becky Tucker

Lent 4, Year A

What, Lord, are you saying to my heart? "Sun of God. I walk with you through darkest valleys. I restore your sight and soul." Thank you, Jesus.

What, Lord, is my response to this? "You are my rod and staff. You lead me to water of stillness and peace." Thank you, Jesus.

What, Lord, do you particularly want me to remember? "Once darkness. Now a child of light. Live in the light, that I may shine on you." Thank you, Jesus. Amen.

Psalm 23; I Samuel 16:1-13; Ephesians 5:(1-7), 8-14; John 9:1-13, (14-27), 28-38

Julia Wepfer

The prayer discipline above was taught by Jane Wolfe at Trinity Episcopal Cathedral.

Ezekiel 37:1-14. *And there was a valley full of bones "and they were very very dry. . . . And he said to me, 'Mortal, can these bones live?' And I answered, 'O Lord God, you know.'"*

Had this been me instead of Ezekiel, I fear I would have answered quickly and without hesitation, "Of course not! These bones are dry and dead. They can't be made to live!"

Often I look at a situation in my own life or someone else's and consider it hopeless. When I learn of a terrible illness or injury, I wish/pray for a swift end to misery via death. I become convinced that the limit of my vision is also the limit of God's power. What a fool I am—over and over again.

I can find no biblical traces of God saying to His people, "Give up. It's hopeless." What I do find throughout the Bible is His breathing life into dry bones and raising those He loves from the grave. I find Him admonishing an ungrateful and disobedient people while still calling them "my people."

God continues to remind me that He is not limited by my poor vision— and neither should I be. He says to the people of Israel, "Behold, I will open your graves and raise you from your graves, O my people; and I will bring you home into the land of Israel. . . . And I will put my spirit within you, and you shall live."

Ours is a God of hope and power, a God as capable of reanimating dry spirits and deadened hearts as easily as He brings life to dry bones and dead bodies.

**Oh God, the next time I see what appears to be a hopeless situation,
let my mind's eye see the valley of dry bones
enfleshed by your Spirit.**

Psalm 130; Romans 6:16-23; John 11:(1-16), 17-44

Linda Walker

Palm Sunday, Year A

Matthew 26:75. *Then Peter remembered what Jesus had said: "Before the cock crows, you will deny me three times." And he went out and wept bitterly.*

When I was an adolescent, I wondered whether or not I would have followed Jesus if I had lived when He did. I think what scared me was knowing how important the church was to me. If someone seemed to be threatening the church, I could imagine myself reacting as the Pharisees did.

Now my attention has turned to Peter, who was so frightened he wouldn't admit knowing Jesus, and the disciples sleeping in the garden. I think about Judas, who must have been absolutely certain he was doing the right thing. I think of Joseph of Arimathea, who carefully cared for Jesus' body, and Pilate, who didn't want to go along with the crowd, but he did. There was also Simon. I wonder if he carried the cross gladly. Mary Magdalene and the other women were the only ones who stood fast throughout, watching and waiting. Which of these am I?

I am not one, but all. I have been and will continue to be each at different times. I have been afraid and denied Christ, if not to others, then to myself. I have gone along with the crowd. I have done my part—offering what I had to offer. I have been certain and wrong. I have been faithful, waiting and watchful.

Jesus knows me as He knew Peter, and He loves me just as He loved Peter. He knows my fears, exhaustion, confusion, misguided convictions and my faithfulness. Knowing me as He does, I am still the disciple He now trusts to tell His story—our story.

Guide us waking, O Lord, and guard us sleeping,
that awake we may watch with Christ
and asleep we may rest in peace.

Psalms 118:19-29, 22:1-21; Isaiah 45:21-25; Philippians 2:5-11; Matthew 26:36-75, 27:1-66

Susan Payne

GRACIOUS GOD, THE COMFORT OF ALL WHO SORROW, THE STRENGTH OF ALL WHO SUFFER... LET THE CRY OF THOSE IN MISERY AND NEED COME TO YOU, THAT THEY MAY FIND YOUR MERCY PRESENT WITH THEM IN ALL THEIR AFFLICTIONS...

Monday of Holy Week, Year A

Psalm 36:5-10. *Thy loving kindness, O Lord, extends to the heavens. Thy faithfulness reaches to the skies. Thy righteousness is like the mountains of God; Thy judgments are like a great deep. O Lord, Thou preservest man and beast. How precious is Thy loving kindness, O God! And the children of men take refuge in the shadow of Thy wings. They drink their fill of the abundance of Thy house; and Thou dost give them to drink of the river of Thy delights. For with Thee is the fountain of life; In Thy light we see light. O continue Thy loving kindness to those who know Thee, and Thy righteousness to the upright in heart.* (New American Standard Bible)

The statements in this psalm fill me with wonder and awe. They are almost more—no, they *are*—more than I can comprehend. Somehow my finite mind cannot understand God's infinite ability to love me and be faithful to me no matter where I am geographically, spiritually or emotionally. I suppose I measure God by my own standards. God's righteousness is like a mighty mountain and His judgments are "like a great deep." In His light, I see light. I feel very small and inadequate in the face of these truths. They remind me of the sentiments of David in Psalm 139:6: "Such knowledge is too wonderful for me. It is too high. I cannot attain to it."

How then shall I embrace these truths? How can they be meaningful, practical and useful to me? How can I stand up in the winds of the power of these statements? —In childlike faith, by not analyzing, measuring or comparing God's ability to my own.

Oh God, help me to not be knocked down by the power of your presence. Instead let me dwell in the security of who you are— My Father—and help me to stand in your presence as a trusting little girl. I want to enjoy the delights of your infinite love. I want to drink of the abundance of your house. I want to have my eyes opened and illumined by your light that lives in me. Thank you. Amen.

Isaiah 42:1-9; Hebrews 11:39-12:3; John 12:1-11

Gay White

Tuesday of Holy Week, Year A

Isaiah 49:1-6. *The Lord called me before I was born. . . . But I said, "I have labored in vain, I have spent my strength for nothing and vanity."* **John 12:37-38, 42-50.** *They did not believe him.*

During these last days before Jesus' death, what went through His mind? John reports that even though He did "all these things," still many did not believe Him. Jesus surely must have remembered the words of Isaiah: "God called me before I was born" (foreshadowing the annunciation to Mary) and "While I was in my mother's womb, God named me . . ." (i.e., gave me my purpose and mission).

Yet, here at the end of Jesus' ministry, having done many acts demonstrating the nature of God's love, still "they didn't believe." He must have cried out with Isaiah: "If God called me, gave me my mission and prepared me as a 'polished arrow,' why haven't I hit the mark? How have I failed so utterly; why do they not believe? Surely I have spent my strength for nothing and vanity."

How many times that question haunts us, especially as we approach our own last days! Has my life made a difference? Does my creativity, birthing, nurturing, loving, seeking wholeness for self and others, listening to and sharing in the world's pain, always pointing to the One who is the source of life and love—is all that "for nothing and vanity"?

We must come to the peace that even Isaiah found in the trust that "yet . . . my cause is with the Lord." In reflecting on what gave Jesus' life meaning, surely it was His transforming influence on others through His great love. Even God "so loved the world. . . ." I am profoundly comforted by that, for as Ann Ulanov suggests, "Women know in their bones the difference they have made in the lives of those they love."*

I *do know* deep within that my love (given by God) has made a difference in some lives, and though the world will never know nor honor (believe), still *I know*, and God knows, and that makes all the difference. At the end, we each can say, "My reward is with my God" (Isaiah 49:4).

Psalm 71:1-12; I Corinthians 1:18-31

Ann Young

* *The Female Ancestors of Christ*, by Ann Belford Ulanov, Shambala Publications, 1993, p. 89

Wednesday of Holy Week, Year A

**Hebrews 9:11-15, 24-28. . . . *How much more will the blood of Christ,
who through the eternal Spirit offered himself without blemish to God,
purify your conscience from dead works to serve the living God.***

The phrase *dead works* grabs me by the throat and won't let go. I keep
thinking about the old stuff I insist on dragging around with me and how it
saps my energy. What a gift to me this sacrifice Christ made, to free my
conscience of dead works so that I can serve the Living God, to serve life,
not dead works! What a lovely, light burden He rests on my shoulders, if
only I could accept it!

The image comes to mind of an old-fashioned roller towel that presents
me with the same old smudged handprints, along with some sticky self-
congratulations smeared along the edges—and, of course, a measure of
black guilt, like tar, that my puny hands cannot scrub away. What I am
being offered with such generosity is a fresh, white towel every moment
of my life.

My recurring myopia is that I see the towel dirty even when it has been
made fresh and white. To see the towel white is an act of hearing as well as
an act of seeing. Once again if I listen to the Spirit, I will have my vision
transformed.

Listen for the Spirit. Accept the gift of life.

Psalms 69:7-15, 22-23; Isaiah 50:4-9a; John 13:21-35

Connie Hollenberg

Maundy Thursday, Year A

I Corinthians 11:23-26, (27-32).

My first memory of an Episcopal Maundy Thursday service was at Christ Church, Little Rock, some 45 years ago. My senses were sharpened by the smell of furniture polish, candle wax, perfume and furs of the Episcopal ladies, and the sight of the altar set for the Eucharist. I was caught up in the magic and mystery of the service.

Afterward came the stripping of the altar, and my mood changed to pensiveness and contemplation. Jesus had celebrated the Passover with His disciples on the night before He was to be crucified and had given the feast a new meaning, which the Church would never forget: Bread and wine would henceforth represent Him, His coming, His work among them and His final gift to them, which was to follow in a few hours.

Martin Thornton reminds us in *A Joyful Heart*, a study of Holy Week, that there are many ways to celebrate that time. Ancient, modern, formal, informal—they all include Maundy Thursday, Good Friday, Holy Saturday and Easter Sunday. Maundy Thursday is basically, according to Thornton, the day of the Eucharistic celebration.

What does the word celebration mean? First, it implies community in that we celebrate in the company of others. Second, it is based on a significant event of the past. Third, the event is more than recalled; it is reenacted. Maundy Thursday points to the family feast of the people of God—the Christian family meal. It is the reenactment of the Passion, which brought to fruition upon the cross the purpose of the Incarnation.

Almighty Father, on the night before Christ was put to death, He instituted the Sacrament of His Body and Blood. Help us to receive these gifts in remembrance of Him and in the hope of His pledge to us, life eternal. In His name we pray. Amen.

Psalms 78:14-20, 23-25; Exodus 12:1-14a; Luke 22:14-30

Mary Ware

Good Friday, Year A

John 19:28. *Jesus knew that by now everything had been completed; and in order to make the scripture come true, He said, "I am thirsty."*

In my work as chaplain-intern at the University of Arkansas Medical Center, I was called recently to the bedside of a dying AIDS patient, a young gay man named John. His mother was beside him, placing a cool cloth on his forehead.

As I leaned close to speak to him, he opened his eyes and said, in a barely discernible voice, "I'm thirsty."

After a sip of water, John looked at his mother and asked, "Mama, are you embarrassed?"

To which she replied, "No, son, I'm not embarrassed. You're my son, and I love you."

"I love you too, Mama. I'm sorry."

"I'm sorry too, son. I'm sorry for all the mean things I've said to you and all the times I left you alone. I didn't understand. But I always came back, didn't I? I always came back. Will you forgive me for leaving you?"

Jesus and John—two young men struck down in the prime of life, two young men suffering rejection and humiliation, two young men forgiving the ones who did them wrong, two mothers weeping for their sons.

Spend some time reflecting on the important relationships in your life. Let God show you where there is need for reconciliation. Ask for His guidance in discerning if there is some action you need to take.

Psalm 40:1-14; Isaiah 52:13-53:12; Hebrews 10:1-25; John 19:1-37

Patsy Daggett

Holy Saturday, Year A

Psalm 130. *If you, O Lord, kept a record of sins, O Lord, who could stand?* (Student's Bible, New International Version)

Why do we tend to keep a mental "list" of every wrong thing someone has done to us or to someone else? When my husband told me almost a year ago that he wanted a divorce, I began to think back to everything that I felt was bad or wrong that he did to me. Why is it so important for us to remember the bad times? If Jesus kept a record of our sins and bad times, who would go with Him on judgment day? Jesus washed away our sins; He cleansed us when He died on the cross. He made us whole.

Is it really hard to forgive someone who has wronged you? I used to think it was. I was so wrapped up in revenge that I plotted different strategies daily! Experience has taught me that not only would I have hurt someone, but I also would have brought harm to myself. To be able to forgive someone for doing wrong, you have to pray about it. I have a suggestion. Talk to the one who created us all.

I have forgiven several people over the years, and I am sure that some also have forgiven me. Just think if Jesus had not forgiven those who made Him carry the cross up that hill—we would all be in trouble!

Pray today that you will have a forgiving heart if you are wronged while going about your daily activities.

Job 14:1-14; I Peter 4:1-8; Matthew 27:57-66

Rochelle Graves

REJOICE ALL AND SING NOW WITH A ROUND EARTH, BRIGHT, FOR THE GLORIOUS SPLENDOR, FOR OUR DARKNESS HAS BEEN VANQUISHED BY OUR ETERNAL KING REJOICE ALLELUIA REJOICE

REJOICE NOW HEAVENLY HOSTS AND CHOIRS OF ANGELS, AND LET YOUR TRUMPETS SHOUT SALVATION

GLAD NOW MOTHER CHURCH AND LET YOUR HOLY COURTS, IN RADIANT LIGHT, RESOUND WITH PRAISES....

FOR THE VICTORY OF OUR MIGHTY KING. REJOICE AND BE

Easter Day, Year A

John 20:1-18. *Jesus said to her, "Mary." She turned and said to Him in Hebrew, "Rab-bo'-ni!"* [which means *Teacher*]

I often find it difficult to remember some people's names. Because of that, I find it powerful to know that God is the One who knows and calls us by name. The name I use for God depends upon my particular relationship with God at the time. That's true for my names for friends; as my relationship with them changes, what I call them may also change.

When I am beginning my prayer time, I usually sit quietly and invite God's presence by name: "O *Holy One*, let me know your presence." The repetition of God's name helps me to focus on our relationship. When I am troubled, I may call *God, Mother* or *Father* and imagine being held and comforted in God's arms. At times of loneliness, my name for God may be *Holy Friend*. As I am walking and rediscovering God's creation, *Creator* seems to best describe how I am relating to God. At times when I am very afraid or feel the presence of evil, I have been able to dispel the fear and the sense of evil by saying the name of God.

We celebrate today for it was on this day that we knew a new name for God: the *Resurrected Christ!* It was on this day that Mary Magdalene was able to proclaim, "I have seen the Lord!" After all the time she had spent with him, she saw clearly who He was only when she saw Him at the empty tomb and He called her by name.

God calls us by name today. We often become frustrated because we do not hear God's voice clearly. We believe that God has forsaken us, that we lack enough faith, that God is absent. But God does continue to call us by name. Perhaps we need to be quiet enough that we can hear God's call. Perhaps we need to call upon God with a name not given to us by others but to really know with whom we are in relationship and call upon God by that name.

Ask yourself what name(s) best describes your relationship with God. What Easter disciplines need to be employed to deepen that relationship?

Acts 10:34-43; Psalm 118:14-29; Colossians 3:1-4

Joyce Hardy

110

Easter 2, Year A

I Peter 1:3-9. *In this you rejoice, even if now for a little while you have had to suffer various trials, so that the genuineness of your faith—being more precious than gold that, though perishable, is tested by fire—may be found to result in praise and glory and honor when Jesus Christ is revealed.*

The problem of suffering was a stumbling block to my faith in my later teens and early twenties. I was angry and railed against a God who could create such a messed-up world, one apparently too powerless to correct Her/His mistakes. If anyone said God brings good from suffering, I would be furious and give them situations of people suffering with no good coming from it. I referred to Hans Kung, who wrote *On Being A Christian*, who said, "God's will is man's well-being." I thought this meant God was against suffering and suffering should not be sought or seen as a blessing.

Twenty years later I have a different perspective. I have lived through some of my own suffering. Sometimes I have been able to bear it. Sometimes I have seen the hand of God bringing meaning into it. I still don't like it or seek it for me or others; yet I can see strengthening in the process.

In Hamlet, Shakespeare describes Ophelia as "one incapable of her own distress." What a powerful phrase! When Jesus was tempted in the wilderness, He was strengthened. He turned to prayer and fasting, and He was tempered in the fire. He was capable of His own distress. He resisted evil, relied on Spirit and was prepared for further ministry.

When we are in a time of suffering, we need prayer, quiet, supportive friends and scripture so we can be capable of our own distress, be strengthened by the suffering and continue to become the vessels of the Spirit we are created to be. May we not seek suffering or glorify suffering but be willing to live the lives we are called to live and bear and be blessed by whatever that path brings.

God, in times of suffering remind us of prayer, fasting, scripture
and supportive friends. Let us support others
who are suffering so they will not be crushed
by their burdens, but be strengthened by your Spirit.

Psalm 111; Acts 2:14a, 22-32; John 20:19-31

Susan Sims Smith

Easter 3, Year A

Luke 24:13-35. *Moreover, some women of our group astounded us. They were at the tomb early this morning, and when they did not find His body there, they came back and told us that they had indeed seen a vision of angels who said that He was alive.*

This year I have had the privilege of being a chalice bearer at St. Margaret's. Last Sunday (Easter 2) my experience was even more powerful. By chance, two other women besides myself went up to assist our priest. For an instant, I felt we were like three women at the empty tomb on Easter morning. We were hearing the words *He has risen* and our job was to let others know the news. As I carried the cup to members of our congregation, I saw joy, sadness, hopelessness and fear in so many eyes. I knew I was only a vessel. I loved giving communion to children. If only we could keep that excitement, newness, wonder, expectation and sense of doing something special I saw in their eyes.

The three of us spoke briefly about the experience afterward. We could barely talk. We had been at the empty tomb and seen something we could not explain and by which we were very moved. I felt the sense of being there, transmitting a transcendent love I dimly knew. We were carrying vessels, and we were used as vessels, even in our "unholy" state. I want to go back next week to receive and view the mystery again. I pray that I will again be changed.

**Be prepared for the miracle, the change which the
Eucharist may make in your life this Sunday.**

Psalm 116; Acts 2:14a, 36-47; I Peter 1:17-23

Joanna Seibert

112

Easter 4, Year A

Acts 6:1-9, 7:2a, 51-60. *You stiff-necked people, uncircumcised in heart and ears, you always resist the Holy Spirit.*

I have a very close friend, a beautiful Christian and loving mother. One day she called with such frustration in her voice. Her two young sons were driving her crazy. She wanted to be caring and understanding, but anger and frustration would come out. Her plate of "community good deeds" was overflowing also. Her body began to rebel against this stress. All the while she continued to *want* to be a good Christian, but praying and listening became harder. There never seemed to be enough time. Then finally her neck gave out—she ended up in a neck brace—her muscles in spasm continually.

During this time she began to go to a Bible study, and her time with the scriptures began to increase. I stopped by one morning to see how she was feeling. As we were talking, she began to cry. She shared with me this passage, which had been her reading for the day: "You stiff-necked people . . . you always resist the Holy Spirit." She looked at me through her tears and said, "That's me! I can't even bow my head to pray, the pain is so great. I now see I have been resisting the Holy Spirit in so many ways."

Her neck pain, frustration and stress did not immediately go away with this revelation; but what has transpired in her life since is not short of a miracle. Again I see how powerful the Word of God is. When we accept the message He has for us, when we accept that He really does talk directly to us through scripture, our lives honestly can begin to change.

When my friend began to give herself over to the Holy Spirit rather than resisting Him, her life began to change. Stress began to leave her body because she was able to say *no* to those things not meant for her by God. Her life began to take on order again rather than chaos.

**Pray for women who volunteer in church, civic,
or school activities that their time is spent productively,
but also that they do not take on more than they can handle.**

Psalm 23; I Peter 2:19-25; John 10:1-10

Sydney Murphy

Easter 5, Year A

Acts 17:1-15. *Paul went in, as was his custom, and . . . argued with them from the scriptures.*

Poor Paul. He was always "arguing, explaining and proving" that Jesus was the risen Christ. Would he have found me similar to those Jews in Thessalonica? I hope that I would have been among the persuaded, but possibly I would not.

Sometimes the spiritual things I want most to attain and understand are the same things I am most combatant about learning. I fight against being malleable, an easy target. I put up a battle so that I may "own" the spiritual gifts that I finally allow to come my way. When I own them, I am able to share and pass them on to others. I am most grateful for those people who are patient with me, those who don't give up and make themselves available for my many questions.

As a young child, I received a small photo of Jesus standing in front of a closed, heavy, wooden door from my Sunday school teacher. I often think of that photograph and its symbolic meaning in my own life. I often pray for an awareness of Christ in my life. God's grace manifests itself in many ways, often in humble, subtle ways, and the more open I am to accepting His grace, the more attuned I become to seeing it in others. No matter how far I depart from Christ, I can always find Him standing at my soul's door.

> **Pray for people who close their door to Christ,**
> **the servants on earth who come in many**
> **guises—especially remembering teen-agers**
> **as they struggle to be creative**
> **and strong in their journey.**

Psalm 66:1-11; I Peter 2:1-10; John 14:1-14

Elaine Williams

Easter 6, Year A

John 15:1-8. *Abide in me as I abide in you.*

I daily pray for God's will in my life. How do I receive it? How do I know it is present? This morning during my prayers, I struggled over my usual over-busy schedule. What should I do? How could I get it all accomplished? This is what came to me. What must you do? What are the things you have no choice about or know you must do? I had to go to a lecture given by a visiting professor I had invited to town. I had to visit a friend in the hospital who would have surgery the next day. These were the two things I knew I must do this day. The others were still choices.

I had another response. Decide what you will do and then go on and live in that decision. I was agonizing over whether I should go in and help my partners. I was not supposed to work, but I knew they were overworked. I also knew I needed the time away from work. Usually whatever I decide, I feel guilty or resentful that I did not do the other. I will work and feel resentful that my partners do not appreciate the sacrifice I have made, or I don't work and feel guilty that I did not help them. This morning my prayers told me to make the decision and then live in it, live in the moment without regret. I made a compromise. I went in and worked until my partners were caught up. I tried not to feel guilty when I left.

I hope each successive day I can practice these principles a little better. I feel as if I have a new lease on life. Life does not seem to be quite the tightrope. I feel a little more peace and "I am surprised by joy."

Pray for God's will in your life today.
Sit quietly and wait for a response.
Be open to a new solution to an old problem.

Psalm 148; Acts 17:22-31; I Peter 3:8-18

Joanna Seibert

Easter 7, Year A

I Peter 4:12-19. *Therefore, let those suffering in accordance with God's will entrust themselves to a faithful Creator, while continuing to do good.*

Not long after we moved into our new home in west Little Rock, an issue arose about which Chris and I had to take an unpopular stand. During a meeting of our property owners' association, a proposal was made that the neighborhood install an electric security gate, which would make our street—a circle—inaccessible to the general public.

Chris immediately rose and stated his opposition to the gate, saying that the message he wanted his neighborhood to send was, *Welcome*, not *Keep out*. It was clear that we were very much in the minority, and those who felt as we did were reluctant to stand and make their position known.

The controversy escalated. We became aware that we were the subject of private discussions that extended beyond our neighborhood. Much of what was reported as being said about us was false and hurtful.

When we became aware that some incorrect and misleading statements about our "coming around" to the idea of the gate were being used to persuade other neighbors to vote for the gate, we felt we had to act. Chris wrote a letter stating our position. We both signed the letter and mailed it to each household on the circle.

A meeting was held shortly thereafter, during which it became clear there would be no gate. Chris was attacked verbally at that meeting by several people. I later received a harassing telephone call from a neighbor.

Neither Chris nor I slept well for several weeks, but we believe we did what was right. We do not want to live behind a gate, and we don't want our children growing up with the symbolism of a gate.

What kept us going was our belief that we were doing the right thing, that to try to become separate from the rest of the city is not only wrong, but counterproductive. We are glad that we made our position known.

**Pray for the wisdom to make sound decisions
and the strength to face opposition.**

Psalm 68:1-20; Acts 1:(1-7), 8-14; Ezekiel 39:21-29; Acts 1:(1-7), 8-14; John 17:1-11

Julie Keller

THE ADVOCATE, THE HOLY SPIRIT, WHOM THE FATHER, WILL SEND IN MY NAME, WILL TEACH YOU EVERYTHING, AND REMIND YOU OF ALL THAT I HAVE SAID TO YOU. PEACE I LEAVE WITH YOU; MY PEACE I GIVE TO YOU.

Day of Pentecost, Year A

Acts 2:1-11. *Parthians, Medes, Elamites, and residents of Mesopotamia, Judea and Cappadocia, Pontus and Asia, Phrygia and Pamphylia, Egypt and the parts of Libya belonging to Cyrene, and visitors from Rome, both Jews and proselytes, Cretans and Arabs—in our own languages we hear them speaking about God's deeds of power.*

Each year, as the lay reader's tongue stumbles and falters at the pronunciation of all these unfamiliar locations, I meditate again on the marvelous specificity of the gospel story. God's good news came to specific people—the Jews. The birth of Jesus happened in a specific city—Bethlehem—at a specific time—while Quirinius was governor of Syria. His ministry was set in specific locations—the hills of Judea, the shore of Lake Galilee, even the Place of the Skull, Golgotha.

And when the apostles first proclaimed the good news, they looked out on the crowd and saw that there were people there from many nations, and they marveled at the number of those strangers who understood the power of the words they were proclaiming. Have you ever wondered about one of those strangers, why he or she happened to be in Jerusalem that day and how that person's life was changed by the apostles' proclamation?

Who are the strangers before us today?
Who are the people we meet whose civilization,
heritage and basic assumptions are radically
different from ours? And how do we demonstrate
the power of God's love in such a way
that those strangers will recognize both the power
and the source of that power?

Psalm 104:25-37; I Corinthians 12:4-13; John 20:19-23

Mary Donovan

Trinity Sunday, Year A

Matthew 28:16-20. *Go therefore and make disciples of all nations.*

What an exciting two years being a member of St. Margaret's, a new Episcopal church presently meeting in a local movie theater. We started with a telemarketing campaign calling more than 15,000 people.

So many happenings: inviting, watching new members come, trying new and old liturgy, keeping old and starting new traditions, Maggie's men, *Fried Green Tomatoes* (our women's group), our first every-member canvass, Christmas Eve at the Jewish temple, picnics, Mardi Gras, services at and with other Episcopal churches, moving to a new movie theater as we grew. Confirmation at the temple, at the movie theater, baptism at the theater, foundation classes, summer celebration, EFM, DOCC. Now we have finished our first building campaign—building the ark—and look forward to actual ground-breaking for a new building.

Friends often ask about our new building. One friend said, "We will be there after you get your building up. You know we're not into building campaigns!" How should we greet those who came after the initial high energy to begin St. Margaret's actual building? Should we treat them differently because they were not there for the "hard work"? Should we feel differently about ourselves because we were there? Do we have more "ownership" in St. Margaret's because we were there from "the start"?

I am reminded of the parable of the laborers in the vineyard. Some came early, some late. They were all paid the same. At our first Easter Eve service, a favorite priest reminded us we were not getting special points for being there so early. We were participating in the privilege of being in the group who were first experiencing the Risen Lord.

At St. Margaret's, we have had the privilege of laboring in the vineyard early. We have had the experience of the Risen Lord Sunday after Sunday, week after week. I am so grateful that by some miracle I heard and answered this call. God has revitalized and changed me by this experience. We all took a chance, and God gave us another chance, a new life! Thanks be to God!

Listen for your call.

Psalm 150; Genesis 1:1-2:3; II Corinthians 13:(5-10), 11-14

Joanna Seibert

Proper 5, Sunday Closest to June 8, Year A

Matthew 9:9-13. *Jesus said, "It is not the healthy who need a doctor, but the sick. . . . Go and learn what this means: 'I desire mercy, not sacrifice, for I have not come to call the righteous, but the sinners.'"*

The church office where I work is also the office for the day school. In the middle of typing the Sunday bulletin one day, I looked up to see my 5-year-old grandson.

"I misbehaved, and my teacher told me to sit in the hall. Do I have to? I told her I was sorry."

My first reaction was dismay that he had misbehaved and then irritation that he had thought he had an "out" since I was the church and school secretary. Then good sense took over. I told him that he should do as his teacher asked.

He was disappointed in my reply and asked, "But don't you love me?"

I assured him I did, that I would always love him, even when I didn't approve of what he had done, and that later in the day I would go with him when he would talk with his teacher.

And I thought about how many times I have asked Jesus to be my "intercessor," asking God to forgive me for my "misbehavior"; yet, He continues to love me, just as I will continue to love my grandson although he will, of course, misbehave again.

> **Pray that we will be patient and forgiving,**
> **not only of our own family, but of others.**
> **Pray that we will acknowledge God's loving mercy**
> **and forgiveness of our own "unwell" moments,**
> **when we need most to know He loves us.**

Hosea 5:15-6:6; Romans 4:13-18; Psalm 50

Jeanie Carter

Proper 6, Sunday Closest to June 15, Year A

Romans 5:6-11. *Since we have now been justified by His blood, how much more shall we be saved from God's wrath through him.*

For 16 springs, we were two poets together in a creative writing class. We agreed on technique and style and made sure we used concrete terms to "show" instead of "tell" in our poetry. We shared much, despite the disparity of age.

However, I discovered I did not really know her when, at age 86, she said, "Nothing has ever shown me concrete evidence of a God." I was appalled that I had sat in a class with her all those years and not known how she believed; yet, I hesitated to speak with her, fearing her will over mine.

She died at 90. Her memorial service was conducted by the owner of an art gallery. Paintings she had done were displayed at the front of the funeral chapel. Her painting and writing were lauded. There was no mention of God. My days are haunted by my own failure to try to "show" God to her in a concrete way.

**Pray that we will be less reticent to express
our own beliefs to others.
Pray for all who have died in the communion
of the Church and for those whose faith
is known to God alone, that with all the saints,
they may have rest in that place
where there is life eternal.**

Psalm 100; Exodus 19:2-8a; Matthew 9:35-10:8, (9-15)

Jeanie Carter

Proper 7, Sunday Closest to June 22, Year A

Matthew 10:(16-23), 24-33. *Everyone therefore who acknowledges me before others, I also will acknowledge before my Father in heaven. . . .*

I have a special admiration for a couple I met this past year. Forsaking all the traditional trappings of the world, the man sought and found a deeper spiritual way of life, and his wife "walked with him." His own family refused to have anything to do with them—acting as if they were involved in something illicit, or at least crazy.

Perhaps, in the beginning, his total involvement in his new walk with Christ may have made him sound unbalanced, but by the time I knew him, he was just an enthusiastic Episcopalian—more devout than most, but perfectly sane. As a couple, they contribute a great deal to the church, not money per se but service whenever and wherever needed and loyalty in attending every service. Any church would delight in having them as members. And all who know them are blessed through the relationship this couple has with God. Like the disciples, they faced unfriendly faces, even mockery at times, and perhaps always will. Yet, through their caring, other people in the church who were not happy Christians learned to have a joy in serving.

Do we think about how our actions and our words influence others? Are we too bashful to confess our Father?

Pray that we will have the courage to be disciples in whatever we do or say. Pray that we will not be discouraged or hurt when others find us "different."

Jeremiah 20:7-13; Romans 5:15-19; Psalm 69:1-18

Jeanie Carter

Proper 8, Sunday Closest to June 29, Year A

Psalm 89:1-18. *I have made a covenant with my chosen one.*

As women, we live divided lives. We often serve everyone except ourselves, feeding others but allowing ourselves to go hungry. Since before our memory, that has been the way of things.

Starving ourselves is not God's way. We are called to serve, but not to the point of emaciating ourselves or our spirits. God's love for us requires —demands—a kind of self-love that is not self-centered, but "self-centering."

Centering ourselves takes time, silence and a willingness to nurture ourselves with the same tenderness with which we would care for the weakest of God's children. Too often serving others at our own expense is a disguised form of control, a way to manipulate others' lives while distracting ourselves from our own weaknesses. This kind of "serving" others is a remarkably insidious kind of addiction that is especially easy to deny because it is cloaked in a show of piety.

Sooner or later the day comes when we can no longer serve anyone because we have forgotten to care for ourselves, and our energy is depleted. This kind of "hitting bottom" is the natural consequence of a divided life.

But it doesn't have to be that way. We are a resurrectional people with the power to live anew. We can choose, through our resurrection, to become dead to sin and dead to the compulsion to hurt ourselves and others. Christ died so that we might live, not in servitude and suffering, but in freedom. Like the three women searching for their Teacher after His death, we can see the cast-off wrappings in the tomb and *choose to leave them there*.

Like those women of courage, we can choose to remember that God's covenant calls us to love in a balanced way. The Lord calls us to die to sin so that we might live, knowing that we cannot love God without loving ourselves.

Yes, we are called to serve God's neediest little ones, but sometimes we find God's neediest little ones in the mirror.

Isaiah 2:10-17; Romans 6:3-11; Matthew 10:34-42

Deb Halter

Proper 9, Sunday Closest to July 6, Year A

Matthew 11:25-30. *Take my yoke upon you, and learn from me; for I am gentle and humble in heart, and you will find rest for your souls. For my yoke is easy, and my burden is light.*

The many times I have been inundated with good works! Cooking hors d'oeuvres for the antique show, visiting a sick friend in the hospital, making peanut brittle for the pantry, serving the chalice at the altar, taking a casserole to the bereaved, a committee meeting at 7 p.m.

"When will it end? When will I find rest? I am so tired, Lord."

I read from Matthew: "Take my yoke upon you for I am gentle and lowly in heart, my yoke is easy, my burden light."

"Lord, have you ever helped with the antique show? Don't you know, Lord, how much money we make that goes for outreach? To help the least of these, Lord—that you said if we helped, we are helping you?

"I am so tired. I am so angry. Where is this easy yoke of yours, Jesus? Where is this light burden of yours, Christ?"

The still, small voice comes, "Who told you that making cheese petit fours is serving me? Who told you that rushing around 18 hours a day was serving me? Who are you serving, my child? My yoke is easy. My burden is light. I am gentle and lowly in heart. Remember my friend, Martha, of Bethany? She had the same idea you have.

"Dear child of mine, what I want from you is time with you. Sit with me, spend time with me.

"Who are you serving, my child? My yoke is easy, my burden is light. Join me as we pray to the Father. Pray for your sisters and brothers. Your work will be revealed to you, and it will not require 18 hours a day. I do not require slavery. That requirement comes from someone else.

"Who are you serving, my child?"

**Pray that women everywhere will discern God's work
from other work.**

Zechariah 9:9-12; Psalm 145; Romans 7:21-8:6.

Nyna Keeton

Proper 10, Sunday Closest to July 13, Year A

Romans 8:9-17. *When we cry "Abba! Father!" it is that very Spirit bearing witness with our spirit that we are children of God and, if children, then heirs of God and joint heirs with Christ. . . .*

I was sitting in the Rollo Hall at Cursillo Ten in July, 1980, when I heard Harold Hedges, lay rector of Cursillo Ten, read the above passage from Romans.

Surely I had heard this before. I had read and heard the scriptures read my entire life, but I had never heard this before. What then was this? Me, a joint heir with Christ? Not me, Lord! A member of your royal household?

In the very beginning was God the Father, the Word and the Holy Spirit. And is it that Holy Spirit that bears witness with our spirit? The Holy Spirit is not misinformed! That Holy Spirit is a part of the Triune God. That Holy Spirit is bearing witness that I, a lowly woman, am right up there a joint heir with Christ! Wow!

There is no power higher than the Holy Spirit, equal with God the Father and equal with the Lord Jesus Christ! If that Holy Spirit says that I am a joint heir with my Lord Jesus Christ, it must be true!

Who sang that song, "Alas, and did my Savior bleed for such a worm as I?" Some misguided soul, perhaps, who didn't know about us royal princesses. Royal heirs with Christ are a far cry from "such a worm as I!"

Bring my royal robe! I will fasten those ermine ties and cry, "*Abba! Father!*" Royal heir that I am, I will fasten those ermine ties and cry, "*Am! Mother!*"

This is not inflation. This is a promise of God, and I know, truly know, that God became incarnate in Jesus so that I, a lowly woman, might become a royal heir with Christ.

This is true.

And this has made all the difference.

**Pray that all women of the world will know that
they are joint heirs with Christ, children of God.**

Isaiah 55:1-5, 10-13; Psalm 65; Matthew 13:1-9, 18-23

Nyna Keeton

Proper 11, Sunday Closest to July 20, Year A

Romans 8:18-25. *But if we hope for what we do not see, we wait for it with patience.*

Most of this week's readings do not strike me as comforting, familiar or enriching. I take exception to them, even. I don't like pointing to other groups, as in this week's psalm, and declaring them less than I. I don't like sniveling and supplicating to a God, with reminders of how faithful and prayerful I have been, and asking for approval. What spouse, parent, friend or God wants that?

I don't like the judgment day described in Matthew, when angels swoop down and gather up the "just," while "children of the wicked one" are in a fiery furnace, wailing and gnashing their teeth.

I'm willing to discuss it, but I think everyone is a child of God and that we who find ourselves on earth have the job of being grateful for that, responsive to that, and being sure that all these children of God find the love that God has for them.

So, we need to love them. And we need to provide experiences for them to feel it and to grow so much with it that they themselves pass it on. It starts with knowing God and loving ourselves. It moves naturally to those around us. God shows us how to extend it further.

I don't think a wicked one put wicked people on earth. If angels swoop down and find unjust among the just, we who might try to number ourselves as righteous have not done our jobs.

That should put all of us in the fiery furnace together—or we could find ourselves together in a beyond that is so filled with non-judgment and unconditional love that none of us could ever have known how to teach it.

That is the reading to which I did relate this week (Romans 8). It's about hope for something we have never seen. I believe there is that time and place and that we cannot come close to imagining it, it is so wonderful. It is surely something to hope for then.

But for now, today, this week, to whom shall we pass along God's love while we're still on this earth together?

Psalm 86; Wisdom 12:13, 16-19; Matthew 13:24-30, 36-43

Starr Mitchell

126

Proper 12, Sunday Closest to July 27, Year A

I Kings 3:5-12. *Give your servant therefore an understanding mind.* . . .

In a dream, Solomon asked for a wise and understanding heart. It made God glad, and Solomon received one. The Bible says what a relief it was to God that the request wasn't the usual—riches, immortality, evil wishes toward enemies—no, none of that, but for a wise and understanding heart. It was a good request.

I have been enriched by knowing wise and understanding hearts. Some outstanding in my memory were in Adolphine, Will, Pauline and Vesta. Their physical bodies are gone now, but the experience of being with them lasts and I can draw on it.

It was an experience of acceptance, of unconditional love. It made me feel boosted into going out and being more of, and the best of, just who I was because they were behind me, appreciating me.

It was an experience of no judgment. If I didn't get by to visit too often, no one was keeping score. There was just gratefulness for my being there.

A visit never contained any touting of their own accomplishments, though in fact their lives on earth were measurably remarkable. They were all leaders or wise participants in fighting the fights that their age presented—on the side of wisdom and understanding, of course.

But there was no boasting. If anything, a wise and understanding heart is pocked with humility—plus wonder, gratefulness, forgiveness. We talked about how they were still learning about life at its most meaningful level and how I was doing the same.

Lord, I am grateful for your putting wise and understanding hearts in my life. Let us all recognize and soak into our own hearts the wisdom from these encounters. It is a wonderful way that you teach us.

Psalm 119:121-136; Romans 8:26-34; Matthew 13:31-33, 44-49a

Starr Mitchell

Proper 13, Sunday Closest to August 3, Year A

Nehemiah 9:16-20. *But they and our ancestors acted presumptuously and stiffened their necks and did not obey your commandments.*

It is a metaphor I had not expected to find from the biblical ages. It is too modern and common a malady now—as close to home as atop my own shoulders. But it happened, and not just to one person, but to a nation. The affliction? A "hardened neck."

According to Nehemiah, a whole nation consciously "hardened their necks." They decided not to acknowledge the gifts from a power that had guided them from an evil land into freedom, then added water from rocks and manna from heaven when there was thirst and hunger. All that, and the ungrateful group "proudly hardened their necks . . . neither were mindful of thy wonders."

When it comes to the "hardened neck" on my own shoulders, it doesn't feel so conscious or deliberate on my part. For me, it's more of a forgetting. I forget. So I fill my life with too much activity, too much worry, forgetting to pace myself, forgetting to focus, forgetting to ask just why I am doing all that I am doing, forgetting to drop it all and be still and know God.

It goes straight to my body. I get overwrought, my neck gets "hardened," and then . . . well, actually I remember; I have to. I am forced to deal with this physical discomfort. I go back to recalling what I have learned about living the way of more peace, more love, more focus and, especially, more gratefulness.

Lord, I never thought about it this way, but thank you. You have so many ways of talking to us, don't you? I am, to my surprise, grateful for my "hardened necks." Each episode brings me back to my wisdom, which is yours.

May we all see our experiences with "hardened necks"
as messages from God and listen, slow down and be grateful.

Psalm 78:1-29; Romans 8:35-39; Matthew 14:13-21

Starr Mitchell

Proper 14, Sunday Closest to August 10, Year A

Matthew 14:22-33. *And after He had dismissed the crowds, He went up the mountain by himself to pray.*

In the movie *Shadowlands*, C. S. Lewis tells us we pray so that we will be changed, not to change God. More and more this seems true for my life. I usually wake each morning with an overwhelming awareness of the things I want to accomplish this day. You might think I was a head of state from my "to do" list! I have tried to recenter my life and ask God to lead me to what I really need to do by Bible reading, meditation and prayer in the morning. I still struggle tremendously, wanting to hurry up and get over this meditation so that I can go on with the business of the day. Sometimes I become so obsessive that I do not even pray or meditate. I become compelled to "act" rather than to "be" and try to make connection to what God might want to communicate to me.

Two friends keep drawing me to intercessory prayer. One friend sends me lists of people to pray for; another speaks about the power of intercessory prayer to our women's group. They both talk about what prayer groups can do for those for whom they pray.

I am experiencing what prayer groups can do for the one who prays. Praying for those on our church's list seems to be the best way to center me to God, to keep me from thinking the world revolves around me. I don't know about the people we pray for, but I am miraculously changed.

For whom do we pray? I pray that I can turn my life over to God. I pray for my character defects that are blocking me from God. I pray for projects which are consuming me. I pray for my family and partners. Our intercessory list at St. Margaret's includes newcomers to our church since we are trying to build a new church in body and spirit. Besides those who are sick, we pray for our vestry and various programs and their participants. This past year I, as many Arkansans, have friends who have gone to Washington to be involved in national politics. Praying for them is my best way of supporting these friends.

**Pray for those on your church's
intercessory list for this week.**

Psalm 29; Jonah 2:1-9; Romans 9:1-5

Joanna Seibert

Proper 15, Sunday Closest to August 17, Year A

Matthew 15:21-28. *I was sent only to the lost sheep of Israel.*

Several times this year I have been given the image of Jesus as the shepherd. It is not just any image; it is specifically the picture of Christ holding a lamb as depicted in the Chapel of the Good Shepherd at the National Cathedral. In my notebook, I find the cover of the *Living Church* from May of last year with the picture of that statue. I had been thinking about the good shepherd, wanted to write about it and saved the picture to remind me of it. In my busyness, I never wrote about it.

Six months later my husband came home from a trip to Washington greatly moved by a visit to the Chapel of the Good Shepherd. He was impressed by the beauty of the statue and how the hands of Christ had been worn by pilgrims touching and holding it. This is the only chapel at the cathedral left open day and night. My husband could barely speak about it. He had shipped home a small wall plaque of the carving. I look at it by my kitchen window as I write to you this wintry morning.

I have had difficulty with biblical images such as the shepherd. It is not part of my society. It is not an everyday image. Sheep are a novelty.

I do know that like the House of Israel and the Canaanite woman, I am lost. Much of my life seems out of control. This particular image of Christ tenderly holding the lost lamb gives me hope. I feel myself held in the arms next to the warm body of a God who goes out of His way to find me and lovingly brings me home. I was given this precious image months ago. I in my busyness ignored it, but Christ kept coming back to me with it in writings, in loved ones, in art and in actual gifts. For this morning I no longer struggle, I rest in His arms.

I have a relationship with God the Father and Mother of us all and God the Holy Spirit, but the person of Jesus Christ has been the most difficult for me to know. I have prayed for this personal relationship that I see in so many others. This morning I know this image of the good shepherd is an answer to years of prayer. I feel so cared for, as I know you are too.

Find an image of the Good Shepherd
and imagine yourself being held in His arms.

Psalm 67; Isaiah 56:1, (2-5), 6-7; Romans 11:13-15, 29-32

Joanna Seibert

Proper 16, Sunday Closest to August 24, Year A

Isaiah 51:1-6. *For the Lord will comfort Zion.* . . .

As I read these lessons, I sit at my kitchen table and look out to the beautiful wintry morning, with bright sunlight sparkling through dripping icicles from tall pine trees. Our cleaning woman comes in. I resent the disturbance. I find a few minutes of peace before my day starts, and it seems immediately interrupted. I want it all—peace and a clean house!

She tells me about her 6-month-old grandson who has just died. My resentments now seem ridiculous.

My best friend just found out she will be a grandmother. I have shared her tremendous joy. Now I cannot even imagine losing a grandbaby. I cannot fathom her grief. Her grandson died on Epiphany. Her daughter's birthday was the next day. She had to help her daughter make the decision to take her baby off the respirator.

For one small minute, I am no longer the center of my world. I see the pain and suffering of someone much too young to be a grandmother who has taken life's blows, felt them and gotten up to go on. She says her work is helping her not to feel the pain all the time. It must be unbearable. She says she does not know what to say to herself, much less others. She is obviously a woman who was there for her daughter, walking beside her all the way.

Pray for Debbie, her daughter and her grandson
and all those who have lost children.

Psalm 138; Romans 11:33-36; Matthew 16:13-20

Joanna Seibert

Proper 17, Sunday Closest to August 31, Year A

Romans 12:1-8. *So we, who are many, are one body in Christ, and individually we are members one of another. We have gifts that differ according to the grace given to us: prophecy, in proportion to faith; ministry, in ministering; the teacher, in teaching; the exhorter, in exhortation; the giver, in generosity; the leader, in diligence; the compassionate, in cheerfulness.*

What a wonderful description of community! First and foremost, we function as one body. The members are dependent upon each other and become one, but there is no loss of individuality. Indeed, individuals are celebrated for contributions possible through no one else. The body owes its existence to the special attributes of each of us, and we belong to one another.

There are few days that my life is not enriched by those around me, that my own efforts are not made more complete by the efforts and actions of others. Family members, co-workers, the nurse's aide at my grandmother's side, friends from school days—each gives to the completeness of community and of my own wholeness.

This interdependence is cause for celebration, cause for thankfulness for living among God's people. On days when I do not celebrate life, most likely I have withdrawn from my role in community and have closed myself to the offerings of others. I am revived and live more wholly when I again allow myself to give and receive.

May we be aware of the gifts given to each of us
and of our need for one another.

Psalm 26; Jeremiah 15:15-21; Matthew 16:21-27

Ann Grimes

Proper 18, Sunday Closest to September 7, Year A

Matthew 18:15-20. *For where two or three are gathered in my name, I am there among them.*

In the last few years, we have watched the walls of communism crumble. My husband and I traveled with another couple through eastern Europe in 1990, amazed at the changes taking place. In Prague, we walked through Wenceslas Square, where countless flowers and letters from throughout the world conveyed congratulations to Czechoslovakians on their new freedom. We chipped concrete from the Berlin wall. We marveled at the restoration already under way on synagogues and churches.

The voice of a network television reporter caught my ear last night, though the screen was not in my line of sight. The story, coming from Moscow, went something like this: "Lenin said that religion was like cheap vodka. How profound was the failure of communism to conquer the Russian soul! Religion was never completely absent from the country, despite communist rule. In the last few years, thousands of Orthodox churches have come back to life."

As the voice continued, my memory called up images of crosses, onion domes, stars of David actually seen on that trip. But more amazing were the pictures I had to imagine—two or three gathered together, quietly and secretly, stretching back across the countryside decade after decade.

**Pray for all who gather together in worship
and pray for understanding
among the peoples of the world.**

Psalm 119:33-48; Ezekiel 33:(1-6), 7-11; Romans 12:9-21

Ann Grimes

Proper 19, Sunday Closest to September 14, Year A

Ecclesiasticus 27:30-28:7. *Anger and wrath, these also are abominations, yet a sinner holds on to them. . . . Does anyone harbor anger against another, and expect healing from the Lord?*

Ten years ago my husband had moved out, and I saw that our marriage would not recover from its many problems. I had a chance encounter with an old, dear friend, who hailed me warmly and inquired about my well-being. My response was to break down and sob that soon I would be joining the ranks of the divorced. He looked at me compassionately and assured me that I would be all right. He certainly calmed me, for clearly he had recovered from similar devastation the previous year.

"I threw myself into my work; I traveled and I went back to church," he said. "At first I just went and sat by myself every Sunday. I had to get over the bitterness. The rage was destroying me."

I had seen him only once in the months after his divorce. I had been appalled at his tormented appearance and at the hostility with which he spoke about what had happened. The restoration was obvious. He was again the attentive, kind man I had formerly known.

I took his advice to heart. Immersion at work was no problem. I was a schoolteacher with a new year starting. Travel had to go to the back burner. But I made Sunday morning church time a priority. The first weeks I simply sat, alternating between numbness and dark anger. Slowly I progressed through my emotions until I put the fury behind me and no longer assigned blame to my divorcing husband. I ceased dwelling on the deterioration of recent years, and I could see that the future was not bleak. Once I let go of anger, healing began.

Pray for those in troubled relationships.

Psalm 103; Romans 14:5-12; Matthew 18:21-35

Ann Grimes

Proper 20, Sunday Closest to September 21, Year A

Matthew 20:1-16. *Thus will the last be first, and the first last.*

As I write, it has been less than two weeks since I celebrated my 80th birthday, and now I'm taking a long look back at what I've done with those years, all that time! Do I believe God regards "length of days" as a prerequisite for a Godly payoff?

I make some kind of connection here with this parable. It indicates there is equal compensation for all who enter into the Lord's vineyard, no matter at what time, no matter the length of service. It is hard not to see this parable as unfair. However what is transparent is that the owner of the vineyard is in charge. It is His, and He calls, and He compensates and He is kind.

Again from my age perspective, I find myself thinking more about death because death and time are wrapped up together. In all honesty, this is not a morbid way to live. Earthly life is transitory. Jesus talked about it all the time as He gave us life's true meaning.

I remember that Bishop R. Bland Mitchell said, "This is our chance." Whatever he meant by that, it is good news for the greatest of us spend-thrifts to know that it isn't too late—because of the merciful judgment of God, maybe, just maybe, the last will be first and the first last.

Who can you thank for showing you
that God is merciful and kind?
Can you this day help someone
to experience His love?

Psalm 145; Jonah 3:10-4:11; Philippians 1:21-27

Virginia Mitchell

Proper 21, Sunday Closest to September 28, Year A

Philippians 2:1-13. *Look to each other's interest and not merely to your own.*

In this letter to the Philippians, St. Paul gives guidelines for what seem to me to be the fruits of a perfect church congregation, what our "common life in Christ" should yield. There should be "loving consolation, sharing of the Spirit, warmth of affection or compassion." He asks the Philippians to fill up his cup of happiness by thinking and feeling alike with the same love for one another.

Eugene Peterson, in his contemporary English translation, *The Message*, puts it this way: "If you've gotten anything at all out of following Christ, if His love has made any difference in your life, if being in a community of the Spirit means anything to you, if you have a heart, if you care—then do me a favor. Agree with each other, love each other, be deep-spirited friends."

Can I really love like that? I still presume to pass judgment on other people, and what am I doing to them and to Jesus? St. Paul asks his new Christians to do all they have to do "without complaint or wrangling," no more "bickering." I do believe there would be less faultfinding in our churches if we could "look to each other's interest" and not merely to our own. I wish I could do that.

I have a friend whose credo is: "Give away one thing a day." Having been a recipient many times, I find she is giving something of herself with whatever she gives, some affection and caring, some evidence of the love that lights up her life.

> **What are you learning of the love of Jesus**
> **through someone close to you?**
> **Try putting that love in action in your life,**
> **in your home or workplace,**
> **or wherever you find yourself this day.**

Psalm 25:1-14; Ezekiel 18:1-4, 25-32

Virginia Mitchell

136

Proper 22, Sunday Closest to October 5, Year A

Philippians 3:14-21. *Only let our conduct be consistent with the level we have already reached.*

There are many times I find myself thinking I was a better Christian long ago than I am now. But I keep trying, trying to grow in love. To be "mature in Christ" is St. Paul's goal for his new Christians: "The prize which is God's call to the life above in Christ Jesus." He offers himself to be the example that they can follow, to be their guide.

It is a blessing to have guides, and I certainly have mine. I have and have had my St. Pauls. They are by no means all octogenarians either! I am always learning something from people who are not even half my age. I have had some of the greatest teachers among members of the clergy of our Episcopal Church. I find myself in unrepayable debt to these servants of God who labor in His vineyard, keeping the church an effective instrument in the world today

How do we say *thank you* to these guides? One way for me would be to let my way of life show more of their influence on it, to let my conduct be consistent with the level of Christian knowledge that they have helped me reach. I like the image of royalty which St. Paul gives to Christians. We are "citizens of heaven," he proclaims!

**Think of three people who have been Christian guides for you.
Are you able to be one for someone this day?**

Psalm 80; Isaiah 5:1-7; Matthew 21:33-43

Virginia Mitchell

Proper 23, Sunday Closest to October 12, Year A

Psalm 23. *The Lord is my shepherd, I shall not want; He makes me lie down in green pastures, He leads me beside still waters; He restores my soul.*

Would you like to have your soul restored? *Restore* means "to make strong or to bring back to health." Surely we would all like for our souls to be made strong.

The Lord made David lie down in green pastures to help restore his soul. I've done that many times early in the summer when the grasses are growing in our pastures faster than the horses can nibble them down. When I lie down, I can feel the dampness of the early morning dew and smell the fragrant, wild native grasses enhanced with wild mint and white clover. I look up into the sky and know that I am looking into heaven.

The Lord also led David beside still waters to strengthen his soul. Our cabin overlooks a small lake, and I can walk around the lake and watch the still waters. Even in the stillness of the water, there is a shimmering like thousands of angel wings touching the surface. The still reflections in the water are of sky and clouds, and again I know that I am seeing part of heaven here on earth.

God called David into this quiet time with him, and He calls us. He wants to share His kingdom on earth with us. He wants to restore our souls.

**This week find a field, park or grassy yard
or look for a lake or pond
and see if the water is really still.
Meditate on God's love and His creation.
Accept the peace and wellness He is offering your soul
and be thankful.**

Isaiah 25:1-9; Philippians 4:4-13; Matthew 22:1-14

Lida Coyne

138

Proper 24, Sunday Closest to October 19, Year A

I Thessalonians 1:1-10. *For we know brethren beloved by God, that He has chosen you.*

When I read these words—*He has chosen you*—chills ran up and down my back, and my brief response was, "Why me, Lord? I'm not worthy" or "I'm not good enough—I don't love my neighbor all the time; I don't always pay attention in church," and the list could go on and on.

I shared these thoughts not too long ago with a young friend who is wise beyond her years in spiritual things, and she had absolutely no patience with my doubts about being chosen for a specific purpose. She said, "That's false pride. Christ died for you; what more do you want Him to do?"

Specifically, the Lord has chosen me along with 30 other women to be a part of Kairos #1 at Tucker Women's Prison. Kairos is somewhat like Cursillo—a three-day short course in Christianity, but aimed at evangelizing the correctional institution from the inside out. Not only did the Lord call me and 30 other women from different backgrounds, but He called 32 very special women in prison to be a part of this. After the three days together, we all knew we had been called by name.

One of the short talks was from our Old Testament lesson for today from Isaiah. One of us spoke intimately with the women and stressed each one was called by our Lord: "I call you by your name," Jesus said. "You may be a number in prison, but that's only for I.D. Your name is written on the palm of my hand. It is tattooed there. It is permanent." These women "received the word with much affliction with joy inspired by the Holy Spirit." One young woman wrote later, "This weekend has been worth coming to prison. For once in my life, I feel like one of God's special chosen people."

Reread this passage. Know that He has chosen you.
Say *yes* when He calls you by name.

Psalm 96:1-9; Isaiah 45:1-7; Matthew 22:15-22

Lida Coyne

Proper 25, Sunday Closest to October 26, Year A

Matthew 22:34-46. *You shall love your neighbor as yourself.*

Out here in the country there is a saying: "Good fences make good neighbors." I'm sure that it has its merits, but also its boundaries—six strands of barbed wire can cause hurts that aren't easily repaired. One of my neighbors has been a constant barb to me. I don't see any way I can "love" him. When he drives down our one-lane gravel road, it's too fast. . . . He always leaves gates open on our pastures.

I thought about him today when I started writing about loving neighbors as we love ourselves. How can I write about it when I can't even practice it? So I took a break and went to town to wash some clothes. My neighbor and a friend came in. They didn't speak; they probably didn't see me. Then it dawned on me that this was my chance to "mend those fences." God was giving me a way to write about this. I prayed, "Lord, love them through me; I can't. Speak to them for me. Smile at them."

As I was leaving, I stopped at the door, walked back up to them, smiled, and said, "Hi, neighbor. I'm not as bad as you think; in fact, some folks say I'm okay. So why not let's start speaking and quit trying to run each other off the road? We may need each other some day." They smiled and agreed that it was a good idea.

I left with tears in my eyes because I knew that the Lord had loved them for me. He did it when I couldn't. And then a voice said, "Okay, now go home and write about this kind of unconditional love you just experienced."

This week pray especially for those "neighbors"—wherever they
may be—that you might have had trouble loving.
Ask the Lord to love them through you.
I promise you'll see good results.

Psalm 1; Exodus 22:21-27; I Thessalonians 2:1-8; Matthew 22:34-46

Lida Coyne

140

Ecclesiasticus 2:1-11. *My child, when you come to serve the Lord, prepare yourself for testing. . . . Consider the generations of old and see: has anyone trusted in the Lord and been disappointed?*

This scripture comes to me as I embark upon the arduous task of taking general ordination examinations. Indeed, in these past five years, I have prepared myself both academically and spiritually. Nonetheless, I am scared and can't help but find myself doubting my ability. I am afraid of embarrassing myself, my parish and my diocese, which sent me to seminary.

Alone I cannot do this. And that's the point, isn't it? God knows that I have put in many hours of prayer and study, and He will be by my side throughout this strenuous week of testing. Moreover, I am reminded of all those who have been tested before me and who trusted in God totally during their trials. Julian of Norwich suffered great illness, and God appeared to her in visions and gave her the gift of spiritual direction. Paul suffered imprisonment, yet continued to preach the gospel and endure for the Lord's sake. Constance and her companions contracted yellow fever while ministering to the sick in Memphis while others fled the city. Martin Luther King, Jr., endured ridicule, persecution and death trying to achieve justice for the disenfranchised in America.

We have many saints who have gone before us to whom we can look as models who were indeed tested and remained faithful in their trust in God. God has never abandoned anyone. No one is considered insignificant. No trouble is too great or too small for God's attention and love. And we are never alone: thousands and thousands of regular people like ourselves have walked with God through their sufferings and have trusted. Their strength coupled with God's and our own will never leave us disappointed.

Pray for those who feel totally abandoned and alone, who are enduring pain silently. Pray that they may find a community of caring Christians to help them.

Psalm 149; Ephesians 1:(11-14), 15-23; Luke 6:20-26 (27-36)

Jo Ann Barker

Proper 26, Sunday Closest to November 2, Year A

Matthew 23:1-12. *The greatest among you will be your servant. All who exalt themselves will be humbled, and all who humble themselves will be exalted.*

In both the prophetic Old Testament lesson and Matthew's gospel, Micah and Jesus warn their people about corruption and hypocrisy. They aren't speaking against strangers and foreigners but against their own, whose lives and leadership are missing one key ingredient that robs them of righteousness and credibility: congruence. What they believe, say and do don't match.

How sad when respected authorities allow opportunities to serve to take them down a path of exaltation rather than a path of humility. Yet congruence is hard in *any* life station.

Where in my environment do I see honest humility bearing powerful, gentle witness to effective servanthood? Is congruence possible in a complicated world whose standards are often so opposite of Gospel?

Shirley is a newly-converted inmate at Tucker Prison. In her barracks, there's an inmate too elderly and feeble to brush her own hair. Without saying anything, Shirley began to do what no one else would do. A correctional officer noted, "You are the last person I expected to help her." Hmmm. What a striking reflection of the humble servant Christ is at work in this new creation, reaching out to another!

Lord, make me a servant for whom your audience
and your approval is all that really matters.

Micah 3:5-12; Psalm 43; I Thessalonians 2:9-13, 17-20

Beverly Roth

142

Proper 27, Sunday Closest to November 9, Year A

Matthew 25:1-13. *The kingdom of heaven will be like ten virgins who took their lamps and went out to meet the bridegroom.*

For years I mistakenly wondered about the parable of the "Selfish Bridesmaids." Surely the Lord isn't asking us not to share with each other!

Thanks be to the Rev. Dave Stoner from Alexander City, Alabama, for credible insight into the mystery: In this life there are *big things* and there are *little things*.

In the little things, certainly we are taught to share and even to share with no expectation of return. Load up the extra wraps in our closet for the local coat drive. Contribute to the community food pantry. We are each and all a part of this world, and we share the responsibility for each other's well-being.

In the big things, however, sharing won't work. When the Bridegroom arrives, we must each and all be ready ourselves. We can't borrow someone else's gift of salvation. We can't rush out and buy a right relationship with God. These are nontransferable preparations the Bridegroom requires of us ourselves.

The Bridegroom's will is for each to be ready. It is our present responsibility and privilege to help prepare those in our circles of influence so that when the Bridegroom appears, none will be found without oil.

> **Lord, there are folks in my church, where I work,**
> **and even in my family, who don't have the Wedding**
> **marked on their life's calendar. Help me show them**
> **where to get their oil while there's still time.**

Amos 5:18-24; Psalm 70; I Thessalonians 4:13-18

Beverly Roth

Proper 28, Sunday Closest to November 16, Year A

Matthew 25:14-15, 19-29. The Parable of the Talents

Three things get my attention in this parable. First, the man who was given only one talent [coin] responded to the Master with fear, not faith. Fear is the answer of a man unsure of whose he is. His response to the Master and to the talent given him cries out for the transforming glimpse of the Master as He really is.

Second, we hear more about "trusting God" than we hear about God trusting us, but trust develops gradually on both sides. The man given five talents didn't get more than the others because he was more gifted, better educated, higher on the socioeconomic ladder or more "churched." He was given more talents because the Master had learned he could be trusted with more. Imagine how the Master's investment in this man would increase over the passage of years!

Third, and above all, this parable speaks of the Master's expectation that we do something with what we are given, that we not "play it safe." Life in Christ requires taking Spirit-nudged risks and investing ourselves beyond ourselves for eternity, not safe-depositing our talents for posterity. How short is posterity, compared to eternity!

> **Lord, may our trust in each other grow daily.**
> **Give me the courage to take risks that bear**
> **the holy presence of a loving Master to my world.**

Zephaniah 1:7, 12-18; Psalm 90; I Thessalonians 5:1-10

Beverly Roth

144

Proper 29, Sunday Closest to November 23, Year A

Ezekiel 34:11-17. *I will seek the lost, and I will bring back the strayed, and I will bind up the crippled, and I will strengthen the weak, and the fat and the strong I will watch over; I will feed them in justice.*

Today's readings remind us that we are the "people of His pasture and the sheep of His hand." We are always under the care of God, who seeks us in all things and at all times.

We are also reminded that Jesus is both God and man, both lamb and shepherd. He is judge of all and God With Us. He is the seeker and the sought. He seeks us not so often in the dramatic call, but in the needs of others—the hungry, the sick, the prisoner. He reaches out with countless opportunities for us to respond to Him.

There is something especially comforting in the verse from Ezekiel that says God will watch over the "fat and the strong." The times when we are most impressed with our own strength may be the times when we are least attentive to God. He is constant, no matter what our condition. When we stop running, or hiding, or being forgetful, He is always there.

**May we this week be mindful of the ways that
God is reaching out to us through people
and situations around us. "I sought the Lord
and afterward I knew, He moved my soul to seek Him
seeking me." (*The Hymnal*, 1982, No. 689)**

Psalm 95:1-7; I Corinthians 15:20-28; Matthew 25:31-46

Mary Janet "Bean" Murray

YEAR B
1996-1997

PURIFY OUR CONSCIENCE ALMIGHTY GOD BY YOUR DAILY VISITATION, THAT YOUR SON JESUS CHRIST

AT HIS COMING MAY FIND IN US A MANSION PREPARED

FOR HIMSELF; WHO LIVES AND REIGNS WITH YOU IN THE UNITY OF THE HOLY SPIRIT, ONE GOD—

Advent 1, Year B

I Corinthians 1:1-9. *God is faithful; by Him you were called into the fellowship of His son, Jesus Christ our Lord.*

We are called to fellowship.

Almost every Sunday morning, I share communion with familiar people. I sit one row in front of a family (three generations). The grandmother (one of the first people I met at this church 33 years ago) is beautiful from the inside out. I welcome her husband's greetings and recall that one physician son served as acolyte when my second child was baptized. I feel many good ties of fellowship with them and with close friends in and out of the visible church. Today I was invited to share communion with a new congregation as they were on retreat near my home.

After spring surgery for a brain tumor, there were transcendent moments of awareness when I prayed that the gift which came to me would travel to those I love on that shimmering, fine-spun web of connectedness, just as they had come to me from who knows where.

Now it is winter. More surgery seems to offer benefits that outweigh risks. It is an informed choice but a heavy one. Just for a moment, I am given a prayer: "Thank you for letting me share your suffering for the world." Do I mean it? Good grief! I don't like suffering. But our lives and bodies change daily. We are called to fellowship in Christ with the entire communion of saints.

> **May grace abound and may there be glimpses**
> **of the fullness of joy as we experience**
> **the steadfastness of God's love.**
> **Thanks be to God.**

Psalm 80; Isaiah 64:1-9a; Mark 13:(24-32), 33-37

Dodi Walton Horne

Isaiah 40:1-11. *Comfort, oh comfort my people. . . . Every valley shall be lifted up and every mountain and hill be made low; the uneven ground shall become level, and the rough places a plain.*

More of us than I could wish have lived a life of mountains and deep valleys, uneven ground and rough places. Painful marks of my dysfunctional family were exciting highs based on half-truths, followed by painful, deep valleys that came, oh, so soon! I struggled for existence on rough, uneven ground. I soared to peaks only to fall into deep valleys without loving security or peace in between.

In my life, the love of God broke through to me in St. Mark's Episcopal Church. The Lord's directive to Isaiah, "Comfort, oh comfort my people," became real to me as I sat in a strange pew in a strange church.

I am that deep valley—a valley of despair. My "never good enough," so long a constant companion, is lifted to level ground. Eventually I came to know that I am "the delight of the Lord." I am that inflated ego that zooms to the highest of hills and mountains—carried away on bloated qualities of greatness. The love of Jesus brings me down to a level plain, to ordinary humanity, with love beyond measure!

Days and months and years pass in the comfort of the Lord. The rough places become plains—slowly, little by little. Never do these rough places in me (or you) become completely level. But ever so slowly the uneven ground in me becomes more level, and so does yours, as we are comforted by God.

**Pray for all the people of the world to know
the true comfort of the Lord.**

Psalm 85; II Peter 3:8-15a, 18; Mark 1:1-8

Nyna Keeton

Advent 3, Year B

Psalm 126. *Let those who wept as they planted gather the harvest with joy.*
Isaiah 65:17-25. *I am making a new earth and a new heaven.*
I Thessalonians 5:12-28. *May God who gives us peace make you holy in every way and keep you, spirit, soul and body free from every fault at the coming of the Lord.*
John 1:6-8, 19-28. *He came to His own country and His own people did not receive Him.*

When Jesus appeared as a roving teacher in Judea and Galilee, there was great expectation among the Jews. Other men appeared claiming to be a messiah. Other men came in God's name, recommending revolution and overthrow of the Roman rule. Other men offered miracles. There was a rumor that if every Jew kept the law for one day, the Messiah would come. John's message was also specific, and for a Jew to be baptized was asking God to cleanse them for receiving their promised king.

After Jesus lived among His people, there was division between those who recognized Him and chose to be new people with God as their Father. Then there were those who rejected a criminal, who was (rightly, their leaders told them) executed.

We still have a choice today: Who is Jesus? Can you believe God raised him from the dead? What does Jesus ask of us? How will we respond to His life and death and ascension? Can we be faithful followers? How will we witness to what we have received?

Remember from time to time today the people who were instrumental in helping you come to faith in Jesus the Christ. Thank God for them and determine with God's help to be of assistance to new Christians.

Anne Fulk

Advent 4, Year B

Luke 1:26-38. *Mary said to the angel: "How can this be, since I am a virgin?" The angel said to her, "The Holy Spirit will come upon you, and the power of the Most High will overshadow you. . . ."*

"But God," we cry out, "how can I do what you ask? I'm too busy, too thin, too fat, not smart enough, unworthy, not good with numbers, afraid to speak out, don't like crowds, need to be home when the kids get home." The excuses pour from us whenever angels appear in our lives.

"Do not be afraid," the angel tells us. "You have found favor." God accepts us unconditionally. We are the ones who find a myriad of reasons not to sit quietly in prayer and meditation, to run carpools incessantly, to sit on numerous committees and commissions or to stay overactive in church affairs—trying to *be* enough.

The Gospel tells us we *are* enough; our jobs are to give up our fears, be still and allow the Holy Spirit to come upon us and allow the Power of the Most High to overshadow us. We are called during this Advent season to give birth to the Godliness within each of us.

This week read the Magnificat,
the Song of Mary, Luke 1:45-55.
Make a daily list of ways you choose
to welcome the Holy Spirit into your life.

Psalm 132; II Samuel 7:4, 8-16; Romans 16:25-27

Pan Adams

Christmas Day, Year B

Titus 3:4-7. *When the kindness and generosity of God our Saviour dawned upon the world, then, not for any good deeds of our own, but because He was merciful. . . ."*

The world seems to choose this time of year to capitalize upon kindness, generosity and good deeds. This worldly enterprise seems to define for us—for me—the meaning of the birth of God into human life.

"My God!, My God!, why have I forsaken you? Why am I so cut off and far away from your love?" Why must I always have to struggle so between your gifts of kindness, generosity and the expectations I've incorporated for myself through years and years of Christmas seasons?

Somewhere deep in my hidden parts, I must feel responsible for creating Christmas for myself, my family, my friends, the poor, lonely, other folks in my community. I realize this is an expectation I hold somewhere within.

This has nothing to do with Incarnation! I am the creature, the receiver, not the creator. Can I possibly receive the gift of God being born a human being—Creator and creature as One? How can I become an open container to receive this kind and generous gift so that it may simply flow through my life to those around me?

Ponder with me these thoughts.

Psalm 96; Isaiah 9:2-4, 6-7; Luke 2:1-14, (15-20)

Merry Helen Hedges

Christmas 1, Year B

John 1:1-18. *The true light that enlightens everyone was coming into the world.*

While visiting my son in Africa, I stayed with him in several game camps. The first evening after tea, a game drive and a late-night dinner, we were given "torches" to carry back to our individual cabins. Our hosts told us that the generator would go off at 10 p.m. and that it would be very dark after that.

I didn't think much about this until I woke up in the middle of the night. I could not see my hand held a few inches from my face. I felt as if I were blind and lost. I didn't remember where I had put the torch. It was a very disorienting experience.

In this country, we seldom experience total darkness. The African night experience gave me a picture of what the world would be like without the true Light, Jesus Christ. We would all feel blind, lost and disoriented. I'm sure it is the way some people must feel who have no hope.

**Watch for an opportunity today to reflect the light of Jesus
to those around you. Surprise someone (friend or stranger)
with an act of love with no strings attached.**

Psalm 147; Isaiah 61:10-62:3; Galatians 3:23-25, 4:4-7

Sandy Finkbeiner

Christmas 2, Year B

Psalm 84. *As they go through the valley of Baca they make it a place of springs.*

I have three adult children. My son and older daughter are gay. When my son told me, my first words to him were, "I love you no matter what." But as this news sank in, I entered an unknown and desolate place. That is how the note in my Bible defines *Baca.*

I became consumed by fear, anger and denial. Could he have AIDS? Could I bear for him to be part of a feared and hated minority group? What did I do to cause his homosexuality?

I began to read about homosexuality, and as my discomfort abated, I met some of my son's gay friends. I talked to other parents of gay people and discovered that we were all plain, ordinary folks. I had learned a lot by the time my daughter told me.

What happened to me while I was in Baca, that unknown and desolate place? Baca was transformed into a place of springs, a source— a source of my realization of the trust my children have in me and their awareness of my unconditional love for them. The key word to me in the above passage is *through.* We go through the valley of Baca. We don't have to stay in this unknown and desolate place. It is a place where we have the opportunity to grow, where we find the springs of new ideas and new opportunities for our life's journey.

Pray for gay people and their families who are coming out of Baca.
Let us rejoice in the diversity of God's creation.

Jeremiah 31:7-14; Ephesians 1:3-6, 15-19a; Matthew 2:13-15, 19-23

Susan May

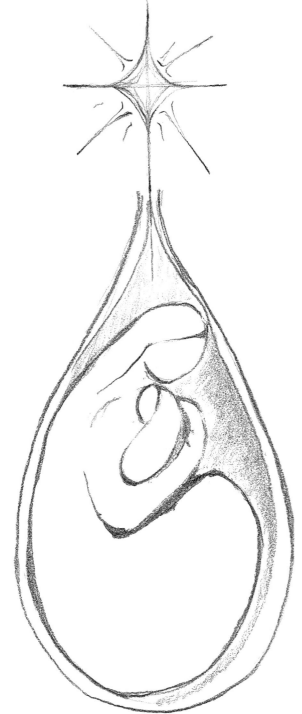

ALMIGHTY GOD, YOU HAVE POURED UPON US THE NEW LIGHT OF YOUR

ENKINDLED IN OUR HEARTS, MAY SHINE FORTH IN OUR LIVES. AMEN.

INCARNATE WORD: GRANT THAT THIS LIGHT,

Epiphany, Year B

Isaiah 60:1-6, 9. *Above you Yahweh now rises and above you His glory appears. The nations come to your light and kings to your dawning brightness. Lift up your eyes and look around, all are assembling and coming toward you, your sons from far away and your daughters being tenderly carried. At this sight you will grow radiant, your heart throbbing and full; since the riches of the sea will flow to you; the wealth of nations come to you.* (The Jerusalem Bible)

Too often in my life I find that my eyes and face are downcast. This is the stance of shame, eyes looking down, head bent. Think of a child who is being called to task, and this is the posture that you will imagine.

As women we are taught to be ashamed. This pattern begins early in our lives and continues to adulthood if we do not have the courage to break the pattern.

This passage in Isaiah calls us to lift our eyes and look around, to experience the glory of the world, to become radiant with our hearts throbbing and full. One of the definitions of the word *radiant* is "to be filled with light, glowing, beaming."

Christ has no face in this world other than ours. I believe we are called to lift our faces from their positions of shame, to reflect fully the light of Christ in our world. Christ calls us to defeat the darkness of self-rejection that contradicts the brightness of the reflection of Christ's light.

Epiphany season is a time for recalling the birth of the light of the world in the ministry of Christ. It is also a time for rededicating ourselves to our own missionary task of continuing the spread of that light. It is a time to begin to practice lifting our eyes that Christ's glory may be revealed to us, that our faces may mirror the brightness of the light of Christ.

**Take note of your posturing as you go through
your daily tasks. Is your head down? Imagine your face
as a mirror. What reflections do others see in your face?**

Psalm 72; Ephesians 3:1-12; Matthew 2:1-12

Karen McClard

Epiphany 1, Year B

Mark 1:7-11. *I have baptized you with water; but He will baptize you with the Holy Spirit.*

Last Sunday two infants, one preadolescent and one young man were baptized at church. All of the young children in the congregation were invited to go to the front of the church to experience this sacrament. The rest of us participated with prayers and our commitment to help these new Christians on their journey—with God's help.

Outwardly this ritual was strikingly different from Jesus' baptism scene described in Mark: We were indoors in a comfortable church; our priest was robed and referred to his prayer book from time to time; there was a baptismal font with clean water; it was a scripted event. This scene jars with my image of the wild man, John the Baptizer, sweaty, smelly, unkempt, splashing around in the murky waters of the Jordan River, dunking people, boldly proclaiming his expectation of the Great One yet to come.

Still, the differences don't cancel the meaning of last Sunday's experience. Yes, we've translated the ritual into our own cultural terms, but the essence remains. There is awesome continuity when the priest, John's successor, splashes water on those new Christians' heads. It's still Jesus, and not the baptizer, who baptizes with the Holy Spirit.

And then what? My mind's voice hears a former professor of mine asking his "so-what-and-who-cares" question. Are these people changed? There was no dove that descended from the ceiling to carry a message from God. The babies didn't even cry. The girl and the young man didn't look new and improved. Does the sacrament work on the baptized or on the family and congregation? Are these four people really changed? Will their lives be any different now that their foreheads have been washed at the font? How will we know?

Too many questions and too inadequate answers—I guess it comes down to faith, the "I believe." If I don't act as if it is so, these are empty actions. If I don't stake my spirituality on it, these are messages without meaning. If I don't say, "I will, with God's help," the ceremony is process without performance. Without faith, it doesn't matter whether Jesus sought John at the Jordan. It's my decision—with God's help.

Psalm 89:1-29; Isaiah 42:1-9; Acts 10:34-38

Deb Meisch

Epiphany 2, Year B

John 1:43-51.

Jesus chose as His closest friends and followers men and women of questionable reputations, with no qualities of leadership and many character flaws. They were the nucleus of His work. He had an incredible faith in people. He saw people for what they were, but also saw that they all had potential. He dedicated himself to helping His friends and followers become what God gave them the potential to be.

I am called to see people in the same eyes as Jesus, the eyes of love. I must be willing to involve and invest myself in helping others along their journey. This doesn't mean that I make others into what I want them to be, but I encourage them to be what God has given them the potential to be. I must be willing to give of myself to them.

Christ believes in me, and other people also believe and support me. How can I do less than pass that belief and support on to someone else?

Pray for support and love as we journey with Christ.

Psalm 63:1-8; I Samuel 3:1-10 (11-20); I Corinthians 6:11b-20

Sammye Dewoody

Mark 1:14-20. *Follow me, and I will make you become fishers of men.*

I never truly understood this statement until I accepted a teaching position in a small, rural school in Northwest Mississippi. Total school population for grades K-9 was only about 200.

The previous year I had lost my faith in God, justifying my rejection with a series of events: My eight-year marriage ended. I was physically assaulted by a student and suffered a debilitating emotional reaction that left me afraid, weak and vulnerable. I was left responsible for a 3-year-old I was financially unable to support without the aid of my parents.

I can truthfully say this time in my life was filled with anxiety. This feeling was compounded the first day of school when I discovered that two faculty members in my building were devoted churchgoers. The last thing I wanted was to be subjected to their judgments and preachings about my marital status, nonparticipation in church activities, vices, etc.

To my amazement, however, I experienced none of the above. I was welcomed and accepted with open arms. Religion, per se, was never mentioned unless I initiated a conversation on the topic. They didn't need to talk about it. They lived it. What I witnessed was a testimonial to their belief in Jesus Christ in everything these two women did. I never heard either one of them say an unkind word about another person. I observed commitment of time, energy and resources; unconditional love; fasting and 24-hour prayer sessions for those in need. Even though both experienced personal losses, adversity, health or financial problems that year, neither lost faith in the Lord.

These dear friends, Cheri Kay and Margie, were truly *fishers of men*. Students watched them closely, many choosing to follow their example of Christian living. Children were not the only ones; I am a living example of one fish that had gotten away, only to be caught again in their nets.

Remember the words of Henry Ward Beecher: "If a man cannot be a Christian in the place where he is, he cannot be a Christian anywhere."

Pray to become "fishers of men" by becoming living testimonials of the teachings of Jesus Christ.

Psalm 130; Jeremiah 3:21-4:2; I Corinthians 7:17-23

Scottie Healy

Epiphany 4, Year B

Mark 1:21-28. *Jesus rebuked him: "Be silent," He said, "and come out of him."*

The man, shrieking and ranting wildly in a synagogue in Capernaum, was possessed by an evil spirit. Jesus knew that the spirit had to be silenced before it could come out of the man and leave him at peace.

Does this sound like exorcism or witchcraft? It helps me to think of it this way: Just as the man from Capernaum did, I must deal with the evil spirits that live inside me—resentment, pride, envy, covetousness, sloth, to name a few. This isn't an easy thing to do, as these dark sides of my nature are continually ranting at me to justify themselves in my own mind: (*She* never phones *me*; so why should I invite her to my house? . . . I've already done my share of volunteer work; now it's somebody else's turn. . . . Apologizing to *him* would be beneath me.)

It's only when I am quiet and still that I can turn to God and ask Him to accept the thoughts of my heart and direct me. A writer for *Forward* explains, "Stillness is not just the absence of noise; it is the presence of myself so God can reach and teach me."

Today I'll try to remember that Christ came to the world on a silent night, when the world lay in solemn stillness and how silently the wondrous gift was given. And I'll heed the words of the psalmist: "Be still and know that I am God."

This week practice being silent—if only for a few minutes a day. Be still, breathe deeply and try to listen.

Psalm 111; Deuteronomy 18:15-20; I Corinthians 8:1b-13

Betty Rowland

Epiphany 5, Year B

II Kings 4:(8-17), 18-21 (22-31), 32-37. *Then the mother of the child said, "As the Lord lives . . . I will not leave without you."*

I had always heard the story of the Shunemite woman and Elisha as an example of a prophetic miracle; but today I am hearing it as an Epiphany story for women. Epiphany is when we show forth the light and abundant life we know because of our connection with God.

This Shunemite woman certainly knows how to let her own light shine. First she invites a strange man to come into her home and eat. Then she decides he is "holy" and makes a guest room for him.

She has a son, as the prophet predicts, and when he dies of sunstroke, she trusts her feelings about the prophet, going to him in her grief. She trusts the prophet to revive her child and He does.

Custom and culture did not permit women of her time to make such decisions. She used the resources of her home in response to her own intuition, and because of her faith and courageous actions, something happened. A miracle that was recorded for all times took place.

There have been many times that I have seen and known what needed to be done—a person who could be praised, a wrong that could be righted, a new idea for getting things done. I've known; but because there were others with more authority, credentials, I have not said or done what was in my heart. I have said, as today's psalmist, "No one cares what I think anyway. My spirit is faint." I've probably got it all wrong.

However, the times when I have listened to my heart and acted on my spiritual insights, as this Shunemite woman did, I have found that God "deals bountifully with me," just as He did with her. I may not always get it right; I may not always be heard; but I always find that I am more alive when I take the actions my heart knows.

**Grant me the grace and courage to trust the spiritual
knowledge you have given me. Let the woman
of this story inspire me today to act on my intuitions
and speak the words of my heart.**

Psalm 142; I Corinthians 9:16-23; Mark 1:29-39

Trudy James

DEAR GOD YOU KNOW WE HAVE NO POWER IN OURSELVES TO HELP OURSELVES KEEP US BOTH OUTWARDLY IN OUR BODIES AND INWARDLY IN OUR SOULS, THAT WE MAY BE DEFENDED FROM ALL ADVERSITIES THAT MAY HAPPEN TO THE BODY, AND FROM EVIL THOUGHTS WHICH MAY ASSAULT THE SOUL.

Ash Wednesday, Year B

Book of Common Prayer, page 265. *Remember that you are but dust, and to dust you shall return.*

"Remember that you are but dust, and to dust you shall return." These are the words the priest says when she or he marks our foreheads with ashes in the sign of the cross every Ash Wednesday.

They remind us that we come from the earth, that our bodies are made up of the same elements as are in the earth and that at our death, our bodies will return to the earth just like all of the living things that God has created.

The ashes on our foreheads remind us that we, like all of creation, belong to the earth, that we, like all of creation, are in the earth and the earth is in us, and that what affects us affects the earth and what affects the earth affects us.

The ashes on our foreheads remind us that we are one with the earth, and the earth is one with God.

The ashes remind us that we are one with God and that nothing can separate us from God—nothing in our lives and nothing in our deaths—not even we ourselves.

Thanks be to God.

Joel 2:1-2, 12-17; II Corinthians 5:20b-6:10; Matthew 6:1-6, 16-21; Psalm 103:8-14

Peggy Hays

Mark 1:9-13. *As Jesus was coming up out of the water He saw heaven being torn open and the Spirit descending on Him like a dove.*

Once on my birthday, I experienced a wonderfully warm feeling coming obviously from God. I became aware of the wonderful gift of life. Driving in my car, I was filled with a sense of well-being and enjoyment. I felt so blessed to be given this gift.

Now my life with Christ makes me aware of the wonderful gift of eternal life, as promised by God and symbolized by the resurrection of Christ. This promise given to me is one I need to accept, take and use. Like a birthday present, I should unwrap it carefully, examine with pleasure, own with delight and use constantly. This gift was paid for by another so that I could have it, not because I am worthy but because I am loved and valued. I will have eternal life filled with this sense of well-being and joy.

The gift of eternal life, with a clear conscience, gives me joy each time I take it out. What we do with our gifts is up to us; perhaps I could take mine out more often.

**Thank you, Lord. I am grateful for all your creation,
seen and unseen. I am in awe of your completeness
in all of your plan. Send me forth with joy.**

I Peter 3:18-22; Genesis 9:8-17, Psalm 25

Jenny Jackson

Lent 2, Year B

Genesis 22:1-14. *You have not held back from me or begrudged giving me your son, your only son.*

The times in my life that have been the most barren and difficult have been those times when I was trying to make something happen. I was so focused on my own will that God's plan for my life meant nothing. I had no intention of asking, trusting or being patient to see what He might have in mind; I was determined to have my own way. How different I was from Abraham, who loved and believed in God's wisdom to the end that he would have sacrificed his own son if God had required that of him!

One thing I have learned through the years and keep learning is that any attempt on my part to force God's plan out of the way so I can have mine ends in disaster. In contrast, the two areas of my life that I gave over most completely to God—the place where I live and the work I do—are so perfect for me that I stand in awe of those blessings daily.

Letting go of our need to control what God sends us can set Him free to send us His best. Trust God to bring you His best in God's time and in God's way.

**If you were to give up trying to control God's plan
for your life, what would you do differently?
Make a list and begin.**

Psalm 16; Romans 8:31-39; Mark 8:31-38

Phyllis Raney

John 2:13-22. *Take these things out of here! Stop making my Father's house a market place!*

What would Jesus say if He walked into the church where we worship today? Would He find Samaritans, Mary Magdalenes, Matthews, maybe even a Judas or two? Or would He find a 20th-century version of Christian phariseeism? What if Jesus came in the form of a gay, black priest from the ghetto? Would He be welcome? What if He came in the form of a manipulative, white, male priest from a well-to-do family? Would He be more welcome?

Does Jesus still become enraged at the desecration of the temple, at blocking the doors in the name of God, allowing entrance only to those who fit the formula? The answer is *yes.*

As women of the 1990s, the doors of the temple have come ajar to us. What should we do if we find ourselves in the midst of desecration of ground we thought would be holy?

We must be careful not to follow our urge to convey the desecration once again within the safety of tradition. Rather, we must keep our hearts open to the sight of the desecration. To do any less would be a discredit to Jesus. To do any less would be a sin, even against the Holy Spirit. It is painful, but we honor Jesus when we look at it and see it. The Church is not God, and God is not the Church.

If you live in a desecrated temple, read Psalm 19.
You will find solace in God there. Jesus did too. Amen.

Psalm 19:7-14; Exodus 20:1-17; Romans 7:13-25

Becky Tucker

Lent 4, Year B

What, Lord, are you saying to my heart? "Weep and pray for my sacred city. Still there is strife and discord in Jerusalem." Thank you, Jesus.

What, Lord, is my response to this? "Blessed are the peacemakers. Harder than feeding the five thousand or tearing down the walls of the city is the healing of hearts." Thank you, Jesus.

What, Lord, do you particularly want me to remember? "Feed my sheep. Heal their hearts. There is enough." Thank you, Jesus. Amen.

Psalm 122; II Chronicles 36:14-23; Ephesians 2:4-10; John 6:4-15

Julia Wepfer

The prayer discipline above was taught by Jane Wolfe at Trinity Episcopal Cathedral.

Lent 5, Year B

Jeremiah 31:31-34. *Behold, the days are coming, says the Lord, when I will make a new covenant with the house of Israel and the house of Judah, not like the covenant which I made with their ancestors when I took them by the hand to bring them out of Egypt, my covenant which they broke, though I was their husband, says the Lord.*

So many times I think that God must be tired of fooling with me, must be ready to wash His hands of me because I've messed up again. When I remember what I've done to hurt God and those He loves, I fear He will abandon me, rub my nose in my sin and tell me how bad I've been. And yet, in today's passage from Jeremiah, there's no hint of God abandoning His people. There's no mention of the hurt they inflicted upon Him.

Instead, God's focus is on a new covenant, not abandonment and retribution. He talks about new terms for the marriage between Him and His people. This time the contract (which He initiates) is going to be different. This time God is going to put His law within His people; He's going to write it upon their hearts. And, as if that were not enough, He's going to forget their sin.

This is magnanimous behavior on the part of a spurned spouse. There are no threats here, no recriminations, no "If you do this again, it's over," just the insistent calling back into relationship by a loving, faithful God.

Teach me, God, to be as giving and forgiving
in my own relationships as you are with me.

Psalm 51; Hebrews 5:(1-4), 5-10; John 12:20-33

Linda Walker

Palm Sunday, Year B

Mark 14:32-15:47. *And He said to His disciples, "Sit here while I pray."*

We are in a season of prayer and preparation. Perhaps we are growing weary of the discipline to which we committed ourselves weeks ago. "Is the yoke I wear easy, or am I wearing it wrong?" is a question posed by Jane Wolfe in spiritual direction. I have focused a lot of attention on myself. Lent is a time of self-examination. My questions have been: What gifts have I been given? Have I been anxiously rushing from one task to another, fending off guilt for all those things I did not get done? Have I been at peace in the center of my being, knowing that I am loved beyond all imagining just as I am? Now that I am aware of my own gifts and needs, I begin to look to the next step of preparation for Easter.

I prepare to shift the focus from myself to Jesus. Jesus invites me to simply sit with Him while He prays. I'll never forget Peggy Bosmyer Campbell's invitation one Palm Sunday. She invited us to participate as fully as possible in Holy Week. Otherwise, she said, simply skipping from Palm Sunday to Easter is like reading the first and final chapters of a great book—you get a lot, but you miss a lot.

Stay with me, Jesus invites us. My prayer this week is that I might make whatever preparations I have to make to spend Holy Week with Jesus. I want to accept the invitation to wait, watch and listen. I want to see and hear what Jesus did, what He said, how He responded to friends, to those who would hurt him, to God, the Father. If I am to respond to Jesus' invitation to sit with him, this will be a week of preparation.

Lord Jesus Christ, prepare me, I pray you. Amen.

Psalm 22:1-11; Isaiah 45:21-25; Philippians 2:5-11

Susan Payne

GRACIOUS GOD, THE COMFORT OF ALL WHO SORROW, THE STRENGTH OF ALL WHO SUFFER... LET THE CRY OF THOSE IN MISERY AND NEED COME TO YOU, THAT THEY MAY FIND YOUR MERCY PRESENT WITH THEM IN ALL THEIR AFFLICTIONS...

Monday of Holy Week, Year B

Hebrews 11:39-12:3. *Therefore, since we have so great a cloud of witnesses surrounding us, let us also lay aside every encumbrance, and the sin which so easily entangles us, and let us run with endurance the race that is set before us, fixing our eyes on Jesus.* (New American Standard Bible)

Several years ago I ran a 5-K race on July 4. The morning of the race was hot and humid—not ideal conditions for running. As I took off at the starting line, many runners whizzed by me. But there were crowds of people on the sidelines cheering us on. I determined that I had to run my race and I must not compare myself with the younger, stronger, faster runners. That would have only frustrated me. I laid that notion aside and ran the race that I had prepared for, keeping my mind on the goal—the finish line! What a swell day! What an enjoyable, even easy race! What joy in victory—for me—crossing the finish line!

And isn't my walk with God the same? I need to train for the walk by spending time with God and in His Word. I must recognize the "witnesses" with whom He has surrounded me and be spurred on by their encouragement. I must not compare my life with others and their walk. I must walk my walk. I must let go of the "things" that trip me, whatever they may be; and above all else, I must keep my eyes on my goal—Jesus—as I walk, yes, run, toward Him.

> **Father, remind me of the absolute necessity**
> **of the discipline that will make me a spiritual athlete.**
> **I look forward to the prize of crossing the finish line**
> **and meeting you face to face! Amen.**

Psalm 36:5-10; Isaiah 42:1-9; John 12:1-11

Gay White

172

Psalm 71:1-12. *In you, O Lord, I take refuge. . . . Do not be far from me.*
Mark 11:15-19. *He entered the temple (meant for prayer). . . . He was*
teaching. . . . And when evening came, Jesus and His disciples went out
of the city.

It's Tuesday of Jesus' last week. He is in the eye of the hurricane. Like a woman beginning labor, the only way out is through His final agony, the furious backside of His opposition, betrayal and death, just three days away.

It's helpful to me to see how Jesus spent this day. One could imagine the temptation to seek refuge in the desert, or to stay in hiding with Mary, Martha and Lazarus. Choosing none of these options, He walked directly into the temple and named the spiritual bankruptcy of the leaders.

With His back to the wall . . . 1) He sought refuge and strength in God through prayer; 2) He continued His regular work—teaching; 3) He remained in the companionship of trusted friends and supporters.

A year ago my dearest friend lay dying. In anguish, I questioned how I could go on living. He said quietly, "Just like you've always done." I expected something more, some discipline of life, some secret word of encouragement. Yet instantly I knew he was referring to the "rock and fortress" on which our lives were grounded .

Those words come back to me as I reflect on Jesus' last days. When the earth was dropping out beneath him, Jesus "kept doing what he'd always done." He sought and trusted the power of God to sustain him.

My dying friend spoke of wisdom that has sustained me, the same wisdom that had enabled him to go through his dying process with grace and peace, and that sustained Jesus in His final days. The secret lay in the fact that this was such an ingrained practice with Jesus, that it was the "natural" thing to do when the crisis came. Is that true of my life? Of yours?

O God, help me to live my days, that when I come to the "eye of
some hurricane" of life or death, I'll know to do what Jesus did, for
it will be what I always do—take refuge in you, continue my minis-
try and remain in the sustaining strength of true friends, that
"company of the saints."

Isaiah 49:1-6; I Corinthians 1:18-31

Ann Young

Wednesday of Holy Week, Year B

John 13:21-35. *A new commandment I give to you, that you love one another; even as I have loved you, that you also love one another. By this everyone will know that you are my disciples, if you have love for one another.*

So we must love one another; that is how we are known. He might as well have said, "Part the Red Sea" or, "Walk on water." It would have been as easy a charge. Can I possibly pay attention with such great care?

I can do all sorts of things—pray, listen, feed the hungry, give to the poor, but to set aside my agenda, my image, both emotional and public and love those closest to me with care and attention unconditionally? Too hard, too daily, too much—too much certainly without first giving over my preconceived ideas of what they should be (my family and friends) and what I should be to myself and to them.

It seems I am back once again to listening for the voice of the Spirit, however I can, on any given day, in whatever the circumstance. For without listening, loving is impossible.

The need to listen is a lesson I am learning slowly and not without a few raps on the knuckles for the sake of emphasis. But it is a lesson I yearn to know, that I must meet with the Spirit regularly, daily. I must do this discipline of discipleship because if I don't my ears and heart lose their sharpness, and in the sudden twists and turns, my life takes me where I no longer have ears that can hear.

Each day listen for the love you bear yourself and others.

Psalms 69:7-15, 22-23; Isaiah 50:4-9a; Hebrews 9:11-15, 24-28

Connie Hollenberg

Maundy Thursday, Year B

Luke 22:14-30.

In the Gospel according to Luke, Jesus told His apostles He had looked forward to celebrating the Passover with them, for it would be the last time until "the Kingdom of God comes." He also told them He would be betrayed, and the guilty party was sitting at the table with them. The apostles immediately forgot what Jesus had told them about the celebration and began to question who was the betrayer and then who was to become the greatest among them.

We have not changed much over the years in that most of us attempt to switch the blame if something goes wrong or we think that we are accused of a mistake. ("It is not my fault. She made me do it.") Jesus interrupted the babbling to say "The greatest among you should be like the youngest, and the one who rules like the one who serves. Who is greater, the one who is at table, or the one who serves? Is it not the one at table? But I am among you as the one who serves."

In Matthew's account we find it written, "Whoever wants to be first must be your slave, just as the Son of Man did not come to be served but to serve." It is in serving people that your Christ-likeness will shine through. This is what will make you first. This is what Christ wants us to hear and believe. Richard Gillard, in "The Servant Song,"* conveys the message well: We must serve, and we must also be ready to be served, to show and become Christ working in us.

"Where cross the crowded ways of life" (*The Hymnal,* 1982, No. 609) the cup of water given in the name of Christ carries His grace.

Father, help us to see Christ in one another
and to be Christ for one another as we serve
and are served in His name. Amen.

Psalms 78:14-20, 23-25; Exodus 12:1-14a; I Corinthians 11:23-26,
(27-32)

Mary Ware

*Cry Hosanna, p. 117

Good Friday, Year B

Psalm 22. *My God, my God, why have you abandoned me? I have cried desperately for help, but still it does not come.*

O Lord, I am so alone. My soul cries for you day and night. I feel like a motherless child. Where are you? This pit I'm in is too deep. I cannot see my way out. Where are you? O Lord, I am afraid. I am afraid of the unknown, the emptiness. My heart is so heavy. Where are you?

My friend Jeanne says that I am in a good place. How can that be? I am so miserable. She says that joy is just a step away from sorrow, that they are twins. And that the emptiness I feel is necessary to make room for something new to be born.

"To learn to love is to be stripped of all love until you are wholly without love because until you have gone naked and afraid into this cold dark place where all love is taken from you, you will not know that you are wholly within love," said Madeleine L'Engle.*

Could it be that what I need to do is to give up the fight, surrender? Then might I learn to sing even at the bottom of the pit? Then might I be able to see even the small signs of God's presence?

O God, I love you; I adore you; I praise you. I know in my deepest heart that you are always with me. I remember the times you have comforted me, your gifts of courage and strength, the joy of your presence and beauty of your creation. I believe that I will experience them again. You have said you would not leave me to face my pain alone, that you would be with me always. I trust in your promises, for you are my God, and I am your servant.

**Pray that you may experience God's joy
even in the midst of pain and sorrow.**

Wisdom 2:12-24; Hebrews 10:1-25; John 19:1-37

Patsy Daggett

*"The Irrational Season," *Crosswicks Journal*, Book 3

Holy Saturday, Year B

Job 14:1-14. *Man born of woman is of few days. . . . Man's days are determined . . . and have set limits he cannot exceed.* (Student's Bible, New International Version)

Since February 1986, I have lost both my maternal and paternal grandparents, my mother's older sister, a step-grandfather and a step-great-grandfather. Last Sunday my maternal great-grandmother had a stroke and is in the hospital. A 23-year-old co-worker is fighting for her life in the hospital with pneumonia. I lost a good friend to illness last October.

My 7-year-old daughter is afraid of dying. I want her to grow emotionally, physically and especially spiritually. I have attempted to explain to her everyone will die someday, even me. I want her to live each day to the fullest. But we all must realize that one day we also will die. We should greet each new day we see as another day that the Lord has blessed us to see. We never know which sunset will be our last.

I am a cloud watcher. This habit started when I was a child. Even now I watch clouds—when I am crossing the street, driving (though this may be dangerous!), whenever I get the chance. Clouds reinforce me. I look at them and remember that God created them, just as He created me and everything I see around me. I see shapes—animals, buildings. I even see people. I look at clouds and see people who have gone to heaven before me. And I know that one day I will join them.

We are human when we mourn the death of a relative or friend. But let us rejoice at the marvel of God's wondrous works—of life and death—and know that one day we will see those loved ones again!

> **Lord, I thank you for all that you have given me**
> **in my life, good times and bad. I pray that you**
> **strengthen me to do your will. And when it is my name**
> **that is called to join you, I pray that I have done**
> **all that you have given me to do.**

Psalm 130; I Peter 4:1-8; Matthew 27:57-66

Rochelle A. Graves

REJOICE ALL AND SING NOW THE ROUND EARTH, BRIGHT, FOR WITH A GLORIOUS SPLENDOR, FOR OUR DARKNESS HAS BEEN VANQUISHED BY OUR ETERNAL KING REJOICE ALLELUIA REJOICE

REJOICE NOW HEAVENLY HOSTS AND CHOIRS OF ANGELS, AND LET YOUR TRUMPETS SHOUT SALVATION

GLAD NOW MOTHER CHURCH AND LET YOUR HOLY COURTS, IN RADIANT LIGHT RESOUND WITH PRAISES....

FOR THE VICTORY OF OUR MIGHTY KING. REJOICE AND BE

Easter Day, Year B

Mark 16:1-8. *And they went out and fled from the tomb; for trembling and astonishment had come upon them; and they said nothing to any one, for they were afraid.*

Alleluia! Christ is Risen! The Lord is Risen indeed! I loudly proclaim the Easter message during the service, even for the rest of that day, perhaps into Easter week. Then I join the women on that first Easter in fleeing from the tomb and not sharing the good news. Of what am I afraid?

I remember my father teaching me early that if something sounds too good to be true, it probably is. The message that Christ overcame death, that we will have real life even after we leave this fragile earth, that we will be united with those who have left before us is so good that I have to wonder if it's really too good to be true.

God has shown us that we can really believe the promise to Isaiah of the heavenly banquet, swallowing of death and wiping away of our tears. We see little evidence in our world today; yet we have a glimpse of the fulfillment of that promise through the resurrection of Jesus Christ.

We continue to see the fulfillment of God's promise to us as we break bread together, rejoice in our relationships and reach out to others to let them know that there is hope in God's promise. In fact, I am able to come closest to really believing in the Easter message when I am proclaiming it to others. How wonderful that my faith can be strengthened by sharing the good news of Christ with others!

In my unbelief, I need to move out of myself and see the divine within those around me. I suspect that this is a part of God's plan as well.

I can continue to live in hope by striving to live the Easter message. When I become afraid, I need only to flee from the empty tomb and run to seek the risen Christ. I pray that I will be able to do that as I acknowledge the divinity within people and the rest of creation, which surrounds me.

This week take some time to observe those in your family and workplace, those you may encounter while shopping, at a ball game, at church. Are you able to see the risen Christ in these people? How does that change how you relate to them?

Isaiah 25:6-9; Psalm 118:14-29; Colossians 3:1-4

Joyce Hardy

Psalm 118:19-24. *The same stone which the builders rejected has become the chief cornerstone.*

So it is as Christ redeems our inner world and rebuilds us as vessels for the Holy Spirit—in our inner world, there is much that has been rejected.

In the early years of life, children start out with vast potential. To become civilized into this culture and to survive in school and family, much is sacrificed.

The psyche tends to contain opposites. Both of these opposites are vast resources from God containing holographic images of the Divine. For example, we are spontaneous and responsible, extroverted and introverted, passionate and rational, obedient and rebellious. Wholeness comes from being able to hold the tension of these opposites.

As children separate from inner resources, these resources still live in the depths of their souls as inner gifts that may later become cornerstones of their lives. For example, a child may cut off from his creativity to focus on the world of logic, reading and computers. Another child cuts off from sensuality to not attract too much attention. An at-risk child who is very bright may cut off from her passion for learning because her peer group makes fun of her.

During the second half of life, these unlived potentials seek re-emergence. Their presence is made known through our nighttime dreams, jealousies and heroes. The energy of Christ is the redemptive energy that seeks to help us reclaim inner "cornerstones." As we find these nuggets of gold in our inner compost heap, we must clean off the mud, suspend our horror and allow Christ to provide the energy for their transformation. In Christ the inner psyche/soul is joined together and grows into a Holy Temple, a dwelling place for God.

What has been rejected in you that seeks to be reclaimed?
Look at your dreams—your jealousies—your heroes.

Acts 3:12a, 13-15, 17-26; I John 5:1-6; John 20:19-31

Susan Sims Smith

Easter 3, Year B

Psalm 98. *He will judge the world with righteousness and the peoples with equity.*

I have worked quite earnestly and prayerfully through the years to shed my habit of judging others. Just about the time I believe I have replaced it with acceptance, it crops up again.

I was aware recently of how unfriendly I believed a friend of our daughter's to be. We were together in many different situations, and I always tried to smile and strike up a conversation. This attempt was repeatedly met with a scowl, grunted remarks and turning away.

One day our daughter said, "You know I feel so sorry for Elizabeth. She has a serious progressive neurological disorder. She can formulate thoughts and words in her head, but she is having increasing difficulty in saying them. She really is scared."

Judgment truly wears many coats in her attempt to search for truth and is often misunderstood.

**Dear Lord, readjust my glasses so that I may be
willing to release my need to judge and replace it
with the awareness that we are all equal in your sight.
There is no blame, for much is neither
right or wrong, it simply "is."
It is only our perspective that makes it any different.
Allow me to accept the "isness" of life. Amen.**

Psalm 98; Acts 4:5-12; Micah 4:1-5; I John 1:1-2:2; Luke 24:36b-48

Jane Roark

Psalm 100. *Make a joyful noise to the Lord, all the lands . . . come into His presence with singing.*

I just came back from spending the weekend with senior high youth from the diocese. Some of us did not know each other very well, and some were close friends. After participating in a few "ice- breaking" games, we gathered around to sing. As I looked around the room, a few were really singing; but most were barely going through the motions. It was obvious that they were inhibited—saying the words but not making much noise.

Later that evening I had a chance to share with them my own experience with singing. I told how my voice was so bad that I was asked to mouth the songs at my church Christmas program when I was 16. Even my husband, who loves me dearly, stands on the opposite side of a room when we sing. As they all began to laugh, the tension seemed to leave their faces.

I felt it was appropriate to share with them a passage from Psalms—how God has such a wonderful sense of humor. I recalled to them the beginning of Psalm 100: "Make a joyful noise. . . ." I was able to share my feelings about this—that God did not say, "Make a beautiful vocal display unto me" but "a joyful noise." To me that means I can sing as much and as loudly as I want because all He wants is for my attitude to be joyful. God does not want only those who have beautiful voices to reach out to Him, but He wants even me.

We began to sing again. The boys lifted their heads; the girls were less self-conscious; and smiles came over their faces. As we began to make a joyful noise, I felt that we were beginning to come into His presence with singing. It was beautiful. Our 20 voices joined together and sounded like a choir of angels. Whether those young people knew it or not, we had entered His courts with praise!

Pray for the youth of your diocese.

Ezekiel 34:1-10; Acts 4:32-37; John 10:11-16

Sydney Murphy

Easter 5, Year B

John 14:15-21. *If you love me, you will keep my commandments. And I will ask the Father, and He will give you another Advocate, to be with you forever.*

This morning I entered the sanctuary and took a seat near the front. I knelt to pray and could not focus my thoughts. Three small children were rustling in the pew in front of me.

I felt desperate to be in touch with God. My mother-in-law was undergoing chemotherapy for lung cancer; my husband was away to be with her. I was suffering some health problems of my own. Our 19-year-old son had moved back home for a short while and was struggling to find his way; and our 17-year-old daughter was simply being 17.

I needed to be quiet, hear and enlist help. The organist worked up to crescendo, and the three youngsters climbed and crawled in front of me. I closed my eyes and silently asked, "Can you hear me? Are you there?"

"Yes, I can hear you," came the voice of the Spirit.

The Counselor (Advocate) of which Jesus speaks unites all believers to God, even amidst chaos. Is it faith that allows this communion? Does God speak to those without faith? Perhaps all that anyone has to do is simply ask, "Are you there?" The response always seems to come, and in that light, life's challenges and tragedies seem of little consequence. The importance of our journey here is to be aware of our eternal journey and seek God's alliance as we walk our path.

Pray for those struggling with faith.
Pray for God to shed a light on their path
so that they may see.

Psalm 66:1-11; Acts 8:26-40; I John 3:(14-17), 18-24

Elaine Williams

Easter 6, Year B

I John 4:7-21. *Let us love one another, because love is from God.*

As the years passed, love became difficult for me due to rejection from family and friends. I began to feel unlovable, that no one loved me and sometimes even God did not.

But our Heavenly Father does love me! And to show He loves me, He sent me a 6-year-old girl who needed a special friend. As our friendship and love grew, I began to change within. I became aware of the Holy Spirit in me; my outlook on life changed.

Now I feel loved because of the love of God within me. My love for Tracy is only a glimpse of God's love for me. He sent His only Son to die on the cross for me. His love is so awesome and unconditional that He loves me even on my bad days. If that is true, I need to learn to show my love for Him by loving all who are created in His image. I must admit that this is a difficult task for me to undertake. It is hard to love someone you do not like. But when I truly pray about it and the Lord reminds me that we are all His children, I realize that it is His love that makes it possible.

**Pray that we see others as brothers and sisters
in Christ and that His love for us
will enable us to love one another.**

Psalm 33; Acts 11:19-38; Isaiah 45:11-13, 18-19; John 15:9-17

Charliss Russ

185

Easter 7, Year B

Exodus 28:1-4, 9-10, 29-30. *You shall make sacred vestments for the glorious adornment of your brother Aaron.*

Among the very few pieces of jewelry that my husband owns is a gold pectoral cross. It is a lovely piece, but the story behind it makes it especially beautiful to both of us.

Chris was a brand-new priest when he was assigned to be vicar of Trinity "On the Hill" Episcopal Church in Van Buren, Arkansas. Moving to Van Buren was an adventure for us. Life in northwest Arkansas is different from our native Little Rock. It's one of the few places on earth where we are categorized as "liberals"!

We weren't sure that we would have anything in common with the people of Van Buren, but the members of the congregation were welcoming and gracious. We made several dear friends during those seven years. It was a rich and rewarding experience, one that we feel blessed to have had.

On our last Sunday at Trinity, Chris and I were called into the parish hall following the worship service to receive a gift from the congregation. I remember the moment at which Chris opened the cross. It was beautiful, but I didn't begin to appreciate its significance until one man stepped forward to explain.

The cross was custom-made. The gold for the piece was obtained by asking each and every person in the congregation to donate an item of gold that they held dear. It contained several rings—I think even one woman's wedding ring, no longer worn—gold pieces, a child's necklace. My favorite part of all was the gold filling from a man's tooth!

Those dear people of Trinity, Van Buren, found the perfect way to enable us to carry them with us always, to hold them close to our hearts. Indeed, they provided my husband with the most "glorious adornment" of all—their love.

Give thanks for those who adorn you gloriously.

Psalms 68:1-20, 47; Acts 1:15-26; I John 5:9-15; Acts 1:15-26; John 17:11b-19

Julie Keller

THE ADVOCATE, THE HOLY SPIRIT, WHOM THE FATHER, WILL SEND IN MY NAME, WILL

TEACH YOU EVERYTHING, AND REMIND YOU OF ALL

THAT I HAVE SAID TO YOU. PEACE I LEAVE WITH YOU; MY PEACE I GIVE TO YOU.

Day of Pentecost, Year B

Isaiah 44:1-8. *Do not fear, or be afraid: have I not told you from of old and declared it? You are my witnesses! Is there any god besides me? There is no other rock; I know not one.*

This meditation is written with a heavy heart for I have just learned that one of my friends has incurable cancer. All the medical remedies have been exhausted; he will die soon. And so I ask myself, what can I say to him? What words can alleviate all the questions, fears and uncertainties that he suddenly faces? And in asking that question of myself, I realize that I face the same uncertainties and fears. I am just more able to avoid them because I'm not counting out the days of a life sentence.

Isaiah seems to know the answer. Speaking out of a profound experience of suffering and loss, Isaiah still proclaims: "There is no other rock; I know not one." Hold to that rock. Cling to it. Focus on it. Do not be afraid. These are easy words to say in the abstract but hard words to wrap around yourself when life is confronted by death. However, if our faith is to have any validity, it must have this ultimate certainty. So listen again to God's promise to Israel and meditate on God's goodness: "I will pour water on the thirsty land and streams on the dry ground; I will pour my spirit upon your descendants, and my blessing on your offspring. They shall spring up like a green tamarisk, like willows by flowing streams."

Psalm 104:25-37; I Corinthians 12:4-13; John 20:19-23

Mary Donovan

Exodus 3:1-6. *Then the angel of the Lord appeared to him in a flame of fire out of a bush.*

Have you had a burning bush experience? Helping to edit this book has been a "burning bush" experience for me. As I began to receive these meditations from women all over Arkansas, I realized I had been handed sacred material. I had been given personal communications with God from all these women. I was awed, scared and excited. I became overwhelmed with what I had received.

What do you do with a burning bush?

1) First of all, give thanks that you were able to recognize it. I know I daily fail to see burning bushes and rainbows that God reveals constantly to us.

2) Next take off your sandals and realize you are on holy ground. This is the scary part—when you realize you are in the presence of something more powerful than you could ever imagine. I become scared, for I know I am in the presence of something to which I cannot come close to measuring up.

3) Read on in Exodus. God does not call us to match the power but to be present in it. God asks only for our presence. God spends some time letting Moses know how he will care for him and his people.

More than 60 beautiful women dared to share their life with their Lord with you and me. What developed was some very sacred material. Let us treat it as such, recognize it and feel the fire in their hearts.

Give thanks this week for the more than 60 women who shared their walk with God with you and me in this book. Let us be empowered to do the same.

Psalm 93; Romans 8:12-17; John 3:1-16

Joanna Seibert

Proper 4, Sunday Closest to June 1, Year B

Deuteronomy 5:6-21. *Honor your father and your mother.*

This commandment is much harder than all the others for me. For most of my adult life, I've kept a wall between my parents and myself. Now as the parent of adult children, I understand the pain my parents must feel from the wall between us, the distance which separates us from one another, the impossibility of intimacy.

What does it mean for me to honor my father and mother, the parents who raised me before the days of Dr. Spock and child psychology, *I'm OK, You're OK*, self-help groups and sensitivity training and "time-out" instead of spanking? They did the best they could with the tools they had, but in the process tried to make me into the person they wanted me to be without understanding the person I was.

That's why I built the wall. Now I'm trying to take it down. I am who I am partly because of and partly in spite of my parents. I want to share with them the real person I am, and I cannot do that behind a wall.

We are moving toward a different phase in our lives. It will soon be my turn to take care of them.

How do I honor them? Perhaps by treating them in the same way I want them to treat me—by recognizing the good they do now and have done, accepting their strengths and weaknesses, affirming them, being willing to share with them the real me and being open to their sharing themselves with me.

We share a common legacy as parents. We share a greater legacy as children of God. In honoring my father and mother, do I make the final affirmation to myself?

Reflect on your parents' contributions to your life.
Seek the gift of gratitude and the healing of forgiveness.

Psalm 81; II Corinthians 4:5-12; Mark 2:23-28

Ginger Crisp

Proper 5, Sunday Closest to June 8, Year B

Mark 3:20-35. *And when His own people heard of this, they went out to take custody of Him; for they were saying, "He has lost His senses."*

Can you just hear this family discussion? "Mom, what has come over Jesus? Doesn't He realize that He cannot just run around the country upsetting people the way He is. Somebody is going to get hurt in these crowds. Doesn't He care how what He is doing affects us? I'm tired of trying to explain to people what I don't even understand. And now, well, this isn't the big city, this is home. We better go get Him and talk some sense into Him."

Jesus' brothers and mother wanted to protect Him. They seemed afraid for Him. Were they also concerned about how Jesus' actions and words reflected on them?

Whenever we try to follow the path that God wants us to follow, we will find opposition. We may find receptivity, but we can be assured that there will be opposition. Sometimes that opposition comes from family and friends who love us and think they know what's best for us. Sometimes the opposition comes from those whose motives grow out of fears and promptings.

It does not matter the source of the opposition. Jesus teaches us to respond appropriately. Jesus responded to the request from His mother and brothers to come, to give up what He was doing and come to them. He responded by staying. Staying was not rejection; staying was an invitation to a different family relationship. It was an invitation to those in the room as well as to His brothers and mother, who waited outside. "Whoever does the will of God, he is my brother and sister and mother."

Jesus knew the will of His Father for His life. He invites us to find that will for our lives and be His brother, sister, mother.

Pray that you will have the wisdom and strength to follow the will of God for your life in the face of the most loving opposition. Pray that you will not be an obstacle to those you love who are trying to do the will of God.

Psalm 130; Genesis 3:1-21; II Corinthians 4:13-18

Elizabeth Crocker

Proper 6, Sunday Closest to June 15, Year B

Psalm 92. *It is a good thing to give thanks to the Lord, and to sing praises to your name, O Most High.*

This was the summer of my cancer, and I have much for which to give thanks. As I walked through the valley of the shadow of that dread disease, the Lord walked with me and held me up when I felt weak. He sent friends to comfort me when I felt lonely and afraid. He gave me music to fill my soul and calm me as I faced the unknowns of surgery and chemotherapy.

With life, there is death. That is a certainty. I do not know whether the cancer still lives within me; but whether it does or not, I know that each new day is a gift from God. And when it is my turn to face death again, I know God will walk down that path with me and be there to receive me at the end.

**Remember to praise God every day for the gift of life
and the other blessings He has given. By focusing on
His gifts, we keep the misfortunes of life in perspective.**

Ezekiel 31:1-6, 10-14; II Corinthians 5:1-10; Mark 4:26-34

Ginger Crisp

Proper 7, Sunday Closest to June 22, Year B

Mark 4:35-41, (5:1-20). *Teacher, do you not care that we are perishing?*

I've been in the boat with Jesus before, gliding along over this small, calm sea. I've basked in the sunshine and counted the blessings of being in relationship with my Lord, families and friends. I've felt safe and loved –but this crossing turns into something very different. Jesus has commanded, "Let us go across to the other side," and here we go. It sounds like a perfect getaway, just Jesus and me and a few select followers. Then terror strikes, and I am overcome with fear as we are battered about by the wind, rain and sea. I drop to my knees and scream, "I'm so afraid!" That is exactly what I did and said when I realized that the flight on which my son was returning home from London had been bombed and he had perished 31,000 feet above Lockerbie, Scotland.

"Teacher, do you not care that we are perishing?" We are already perishing—not from drowning, but from the *fear* of drowning in a hostile sea, in a world that is so cruel. God recognizes our fears, though, and calms the sea, restores peace—sometimes over a long period of time in which we cling only to God, acknowledging our complete dependence on God's healing words, touch and presence in our lives and hearts.

"Jesus, Healer of our souls and lives, we lift to you all our fears—of not doing your will, of the loss of loved ones, of health that fails, of violence in our lives, in our communities, and in the world—and of our own death. Help us to let go and cry out to you. Help us to let others see that you are our strength and our courage."

**Pray that we will bring our fears to God
that we may be filled with faith and peace.
Pray for those living in terror throughout the world.**

Psalm 107:1-3, 23-32; Job 38:1-11, 16-18; II Corinthians 5:14-21

Caroline Sneed

Proper 8, Sunday Closest to June 29, Year B

Psalm 112. *Happy are those who fear the Lord. Who greatly delight in His commandments. . . . They are not afraid of evil tidings; their hearts are firm, secure in the Lord.*

Here we are again—fear from another vantage point. So much is said about fear in scripture, and it all speaks to me. I've had these nagging fears all my life that are not the same, or as apparent, as those which threaten to swamp my boat. These fears sneak up on me in the middle of the night. I awaken and feel alone, vulnerable, uneasy and very small in this universe.

Or I undertake something such as writing a few meditations for this booklet and I put it off. Deep down I'm afraid that it (I) won't be good enough and that once I expose my humanity and fears, I can never pretend to be fearless again.

So many of these fears have to do with my relationships with other people. The expectations that I've placed on myself drive the fear of being "found out." What's really weird about this is the people who know me have already "found out" and care for me still.

This psalm goes on to tell me how to get to the place where there is no fear in my life, how to live a life of righteousness. It seems pretty demanding. I jokingly said in January that my new year's resolution was to be "perfect." Luckily, though, early on January 1, I had already broken that resolution and am now able to spend this year letting God be perfect and me be saved.

> **Pray that we may acknowledge our nagging fears**
> **to God, ourselves, and a few trusted others**
> **and let God work in our lives to bring us into**
> **a right relationship, into righteousness.**

Deuteronomy 15:7-11; II Corinthians 8:1-9, 13-15; Mark 5:22-24, 35b-43

Caroline Sneed

Proper 9, Sunday Closest to July 6, Year B

Mark 6:1-6. *Prophets are not without honor, except in their hometown, and among their own kin, and in their own house.*

For me to understand why Jesus bothered to even go to Nazareth, I've got to remember that Mary and His brothers had earlier made the long trip to where Jesus was teaching and healing "to restrain Him, for people were saying, 'He has gone out of His mind'" (Mark 21).

What a blow! Jesus had rejected them, saying, "Who are my mother and brothers?" (Mark 34).

Everything in me identifies with the sorrow Jesus must have felt—that Mary must have felt. Such estrangement! After getting over the shock of having His family buy into the rumors of His mental state, Jesus wanted to go to Nazareth to put things right (my imagining). Wouldn't we have done the same? Friction in the family is just too painful to hold on to for very long. Jesus also had another mission, which included Nazareth. With His insight, He must have known that He was not in for a hero's welcome. He was still the carpenter's son, and that's the way His hometown wanted it.

Years ago after I had moved away from my hometown, I had recurring dreams that I was moving back. These weren't pleasant dreams. In them I was expected to be the little girl, teen-ager, young woman I had been. But I had changed, grown in many ways and couldn't go back to being the person I was at any other time in my life, even in my dreams.

**Pray that as we continue to grow and change
in response to God's love, we will release
what is past and live fully as more mature Christians.**

Psalm 123; Ezekiel 2:1-7, II Corinthians 12:2-10

Caroline Sneed

Proper 10, Sunday Closest to July 13, Year B

Amos 7:7. *He showed me: behold, the Lord was standing beside a wall built with a plumb line, with a plumb line in his hand.*

This verse in Amos brings to my mind such a clear picture of what was happening on that day. I can see the old wall of that time that was built to be straight not by merely "eyeballing" it, but by utilizing tools to ensure its vertical line. And the same tool was used again over the years to make sure it remained straight. Here is the Lord, not just using His eye to judge, although He undoubtedly could have done so easily, but proving or disproving to everyone that the wall was vertical by the use of a tool.

This has given me some thoughts about checking the straightness of the walls that I build in my own life. I am a homemaker with three children, and the summer is a wonderful time for me. The children don't have a schedule that takes an air traffic controller to manage, which frees a lot of my time. It is a time to relax and regroup, taking measurement of what has happened during the last year and planning for the next.

It occurs to me after reflection on this verse in Amos, that some attention should be given to the plumb line that I am using. Whether my walls that I check today are my children, my relationship with my husband, God or others, I need to make sure I am using the plumb line that shows a true measure of vertical growth. Are my walls measured by God's tools, my tools or society's tools? I have a feeling from this verse in Amos that our Lord will be using His own tools to evaluate whether my walls are plumb.

**The best way I know to find God's tools is to learn His words
from the Bible, feel His presence through others
and commune with Him in worship and sacraments.
Take a measure of your walls today.**

Psalm 85; Amos 7:7-15; Ephesians 1:1-14; Mark 6:30-44

Mary Kumpuris

Proper 11, Sunday Closest to July 20, Year B

Mark 6:30-44. *As He went ashore He saw a great throng, and He had compassion on them, because they were like sheep without a shepherd; and He began to teach them many things.*

I have always loved the image depicted in children's story books, stained glass windows, sculpture and art of Jesus as a shepherd. There is something so comforting about the kind and capable caretaker who has nothing but your own best interests in mind.

In the above verse, Jesus felt sorry for those who were aimlessly milling around; so He herded them together and began to teach them. He fed their minds and later their bodies as well. It must have been a wonderful experience for all those lucky enough to be present.

I have been wondering if I would recognize a modern-day shepherd. There are people with whom I come in contact daily who are shepherds in one way or another. I know those who generously give their time and skills to help others just because it will make the recipient's life better. And I know those who give their money for the betterment of others. But when I think of a shepherd, I think of one who personally loves and knows each individual in his or her care (even before they are in his or her care) and instinctively thinks of them before himself or herself. Do I know any of those shepherds today?

I know I have not found Christ walking around the earth today. Until He comes to our world again, I can only find those who have pieces of Him that they share with me. And I can only hope to find a little of Him in me that I might give to another. If I focus on the shepherd metaphor during the day, I find pieces of the kind and capable Jesus where I didn't notice them before. And I find my response to those shepherds also altered.

**Today look for the shepherd in those
whom you meet or know.**

Psalm 22:22-30; Isaiah 57:14b-21; Ephesians 2:11-22; Mark 6:30-44

Mary Kumpuris

Proper 12, Sunday Closest to July 27, Year B

II Kings 2:1-8. *But Elisha said, "As the Lord lives, and as you yourself live, I will not leave you."*

The readings for this day are so full of the miraculous hand of God. The psalm begins by recalling the incredible Exodus and then changes tense to illustrate the hand of God still at work in the poet's time. Mark also illustrates God's miracles as Jesus walks on water. Both speak of God's dominion over nature.

But what speaks to my heart is the beautiful passage revealing the relationship of Elijah and Elisha. The overt connection is that of master and servant, but there is clearly more that binds them. Elijah three times entreats his servant to look to his own comfort and remain behind on the long journeys, and each time Elisha refuses to be parted from him. How painful it must have been to be reminded by those at each destination that Elijah would soon be taken from him!

It reminds me of the love Ruth had for Naomi. Both Elisha and Ruth quietly stated their intention to remain steadfast as long as their companion lived.

I have been thinking of how miraculous this love is, and yet I believe it is a miracle that is possible for each of us every day. The ability to simply abide each day with another is something quite common, so common that we would hardly consider it in any way a miracle. I am sure Elisha found the journey to be physically exhausting and probably, at some point on the road, ran short of interesting conversation. But he remained with Elijah and shared that painful experience. Whether it be a communion of the flesh or of the spirit, I find my relationships deepen when I concentrate on that constant abiding love illustrated here.

Take five minutes at the beginning, middle and end
of this day to feel that miraculous love available to us all
as we quiet ourselves in communion with another.

Psalm 114; II Kings 2:1-15; Ephesians 4:1-7, 11-16; Mark 6:45-52

Mary Kumpuris

Proper 13, Sunday Closest to August 3, Year B

Exodus 16:2-4, 9-15. *Then Moses said . . . "Draw near to the Lord ."*

Exodus: the story of an ancient tribe wandering in the desert or my own reality? Can I trust my inner Moses, who urges me to move out from where I'm comfortable? What's the wilderness I fear? And what about my getting fed the food of angels?

Trying to respond to a tiny inner voice several years ago, I quit a comfortable job and enrolled in graduate school. I soon learned that the Promised Land doesn't lie just on the other side of the decision to leave Egypt. My time in classes and apprenticeship seemed like years in the desert—frustrating, boring, dry, lonely. Did I "murmur"? You better believe I murmured. My inner critics, like those folks following Moses who longed for the good old days, were screaming, "Now look at the mess you done got us into!" But, when things looked the bleakest, I was given what I needed to survive.

Is this an only-once-in-a-lifetime experience? I don't think so. Invitations to take a risk come every day—such as an invitation to trust our hearts or to speak our own truth instead of passively adapting to the dictates of whatever collective we project our authority onto. If we listen, we can hear the invitation to leave our comfortable Egypts. We might fear a wilderness of conflict or rejection on the other side of that decision. But the promise is there too—the food of angels. We will be sustained.

Trust the promise.
Pray that you'll be willing to take the risk.

Psalm 78:1-25; Ephesians 4:17-25; John 6:24-35

Sue Campbell

Proper 14, Sunday Closest to August 10, Year B

John 6:37-51. *No one can come to me unless drawn by the Father who sent me. . . .*

Being drawn by God! I never thought I knew how that felt, although I've long admired people who knew they had a "calling." For years I discounted that kind of experience for myself. It could be I was listening for the wrong voice.

The Bible tells us of God's using angels long ago to pass along His directives to people. But I've never seen an angel (that I recognized at the time).

When a mid-life crisis hit several years ago and the prospect of changing careers beckoned, I would have welcomed a clear angel-message. All I got was a yearning in my heart that pleaded for one particular career. Automatically I chided myself, "Put away such foolishness! Now get back to business."

After months of research, reading, talking and praying, I felt no closer to a career decision than when I first started. Quite by accident, I ran across a list of daydreams I had drawn up earlier. There at the top of the list was the career urged by my heart.

It was then I finally paid attention. "You don't suppose that God's calling and my own yearning might be the same thing? "I finally asked, "Could my heart's wish be a message from an angel?" Good questions. My whole life has changed with the answers.

Pray that you'll be willing to hear God's voice coming from even the most unlikely source—your own heart.

Psalm 34; Deuteronomy 8:1-10; Ephesians 4:(25-29), 30-5:2

Sue Campbell

Proper 15, Sunday Closest to August 17, Year B

Proverbs 9:1-6. *To those without sense she says, . . . "Leave simpleness and live, and walk in the way of insight."*

How appealing is this request from Wisdom, the feminine aspect of God! Why, She's prepared a feast for us and wants us to join Her! It sounds so lovely when you read the selection as poetic words about a heavenly banquet in an ancient book of sacred writings.

But will I still think it's lovely when I realize this passage might be about urging me to become conscious: conscious of my carefully constructed persona; conscious of shadow parts of myself I'd rather keep hidden (even from me); conscious of my wounds and woundings? Somehow that doesn't sound much like a feast—sounds unpleasant. It would be so much easier to go on thinking that I'm not a complex being. It would mean looking inside at *all* of me, and then *admitting* it (to an analyst, priest, or even myself). Not simple. Not fun.

But Wisdom whispers a promise to us, along with Her invitation: "And live!" She's talking not about physical life, but *true* life. She's promising that our work at trying to know ourselves (insight) will lead us to an experience of life we can't even imagine in our "simpleness." Far from being a selfish endeavor, this invitation to consciousness comes from God Herself.

Pray that you'll accept.

Psalm 147; Ephesians 5:15-20; John 6:53-59

Sue Campbell

Proper 16, Sunday Closest to August 24, Year B

Joshua 24:1-2a, 14-25. *God forbid that we should forsake the Lord to worship other gods.*
John 6:60-69. *So Jesus asked the Twelve, "Do you want to leave me also?"*

My mother suddenly died on Christmas morning. A fruit salad she had made for our Christmas brunch was chilling in the refrigerator. Presents to and from her lay under the tree. I felt like a character from a Greek tragedy being mocked by the gods. Yet, the despair and outrage lasted only momentarily. I could not sustain any real anger at God.

Peggy Bosmyer-Campbell called later in the day and said, "I know it happened on Christmas. It's hard, real hard. But realize when you can that He is her gift today." Suddenly I realized what a great gift she had been given, God Himself, paradise—a better gift even than the red hat I had finally found to go with her red cashmere coat.

People have asked me if Christmas will now be ruined. No, I'm beginning to see that day as God does: celebration amidst pain, birth side by side with death, excess and plenty surrounded by poverty and depravation, happy reunions for some and loneliness and isolation for others.

Christmas ruined? No, made real. And what better person to teach me than my mother, known for her honesty, sense of humor and disdain for excess, phoniness and pretense? She and God have stripped Christmas of all its idolatry and brought it home to me clean, holy and pure.

How could I turn away from you, Lord? I have come too far. I have no other place to go.

Try this week to strip the idols from your life
and fear not pain and adversity.
They are part of the dance.

Psalm 16; Ephesians 5:21-33

Claudia Howe

Proper 17, Sunday Closest to August 31, Year B

Ephesians 6:10-20. *Put on all the armor which God provides, so that you may be able to stand firm against the devices of the devil. Fasten on the belt of truth; for coat of mail put on integrity; let the shoes on your feet be the gospel of peace, to give you firm footing; and with all of these take up the shield of faith.*

God consistently confronts my prejudices with humor and unlikely messengers. I was at Camp Mitchell, trying to select a reading to be acted out by retarded adult campers at Vespers. A young Baptist maintenance worker pulled up in his truck: "Here's some scripture you might like. We done it in our church, and it come off good."

I don't like messages from outsiders delivered in substandard English. I accepted the reading but wondered, "Could the campers understand the symbols in the verses? Could they convey its powerful message?"

After I read the passage to the group, a camper squealed, "God told me in a dream last night that I'd get to scare off the devil!" I watched as she explained the reading to the others. They beamed as she devised costumes for their armor of Christ-faith, truth, peace and integrity and grasped each one's symbolism and significance. She also directed them in a lively, liturgical dance to, "Shut de do', keep out the devil." As I watched them perform perfectly that night under her direction, not mine, I knew I had witnessed integrity and truth.

Pray that you open up to unlikely messengers,
who may come your way.

Deuteronomy 4:1-9; Mark 7:1-8, 14-15, 21-23; Psalm 15

Claudia Howe

Proper 18, Sunday Closest to September 7, Year B

Mark 7:31-37. *With that his ears were opened, and at the same time the impediment was removed, and he spoke plainly.*

I like justice, especially when I feel justified. I like it when people know I have been right, acknowledge that and the ledger sheet ends up balanced. However, I am finding that relationships aren't always logical and orderly; and most of all, they aren't usually balanced at all times.

Recently I approached someone to work out a conflict we had. I was expecting an apology. Instead, I got a tongue-lashing. I simply could not get the other person to see my side.

Frustrated, I began to pray. I heard, "Claudia, do you want to be right or have a relationship?"

Jesus opened my ears. I no longer heard this person being illogical or uncompromising. Instead, I heard him saying how hurt he was and how he could not deal with my pain at this time.

I did not feel any need to analyze or justify this situation. I knew it was just time to listen and say what I really wanted him to know. I was able to simply say, "You are important to me. I care about you. I want us to have a relationship. I am sorry for the pain I caused."

So many times a need to control or be right keeps me from really hearing others. Just as in the scripture, I speak with impediments because I cannot hear. I hear sarcasm, criticism and illogical reasonings when someone may be asking to be loved or affirmed.

**Pray that your ears be open today so that your speech
does not impede God's healing love.**

Isaiah 35:4-7a; James 1:17-27; Psalm 146

Claudia Howe

Proper 19, Sunday Closest to September 14, Year B

James 2:1-5, 8-10, 14-18. *Thou shalt love thy neighbor as thyself.*

We are spending our first holiday away from home in a northern city with our daughter and her family. A wonderful new friend of theirs invites us for a holiday feast. I find myself in one of the rooms with three strangers also invited as guests. At first I feel hesitant to try to begin a conversation. Becoming aware of the innate loneliness in all of us at times, I realize I am once again becoming too quick to judge other people. I decide to try to use the power within myself to know them. I feel a gentle push in my conscience to open myself to them. We have much to share. One of them has just lost a husband; and one, a father.

Strangers? No longer. We will never see each other again, but we will remember that one evening of knowing and loving each other. A coincidence we were brought together? I think not. Perhaps one of our angels gently led us into Christ's presence.

**Seek to know a stranger and know
he or she is probably doing the best
he or she can at that moment.**

Psalm 116; Isaiah 50:4-9; Mark 8:27-38

Joanne Meadors

Proper 20, Sunday Closest to September 21, Year B

Mark 9:30-37. *Whosoever shall receive one of these children in my name, receiveth me. . . .*

I am a docent at the Arkansas Arts Center. Last year we had a lovely exhibit of paintings from the 18th-century Italian Gandolfi family. I was surprised at the number of children who did not know who the figures were in the paintings of the Holy family.

I ask God to show me what to do each day. I wonder if I fail to see what is placed in front of me. Do I spend enough time teaching my grandchildren about the Holy family and what it means? Or does that get lost in the busyness of everyday life? Am I giving myself the time to see the Christ within? If not, I might miss a profound truth.

I once noticed a woman at a retreat whose eyes sparkled with joy and shone with love. I wondered why, and later she said that she had been raised in an orphanage and was told and believed she was very important because she was a child of God.

**I pray that today I will take the time to help a child
understand that he or she is important
because he or she is a child of God.
Do I truly believe I am a child of God or do I forget?**

Psalm 54; Wisdom 1:16-2:1; James 3:16-4:6

Joanne Meadors

206

Proper 21, Sunday Closest to September 28, Year B

Numbers 11:4-6, 10-16, 24-29. *Moses said, "I am not able to carry this people alone, the burden is too heavy."*

Feel as if you are pulled in many different directions? Running on a treadmill going nowhere? Carrying all of your burdens alone?

Many people have told me that they feel like this. To be honest, I frequently feel this way. Then I encounter a Bible lesson such as the one for this Sunday. God calls us to share our load with Him and others. Moses told God that he could not do it all alone, and God shared Moses' load with 70 other people. Our Lord called us to Christian community while we were still Jews wandering in the desert.

I find it hard to break the bonds of over-commitment. I do not know who will do the job if I do not. However, someone always comes forward. He or she may not do it the way I would, but the task is always successfully accomplished.

It is so easy to believe that if we are doing "church-work," we are doing God's will. Moses did and he suffered burnout. So will we unless we ask for God's help. If church-work fills all our time, is that God's will for us?

In the letter to James we read, "Submit yourselves to God." This includes quiet time, be-still time, time alone with God, time to listen to God and time to discern His will. With all he had to do, Moses stopped and talked with the Lord. Moses prayed. The Lord answered his prayer by sharing his burden with others.

We need not go it alone. We need not do it all. We are called as Christians to share with others, not only ours gifts, but our burdens too. I have often found that a task that is a burden to me is another person's gift and is easy for them. When I share my load, I find that I am back on God's path, walking a steady, easy pace.

**This week set time aside for just you and God and listen.
Maybe He will share your burdens with others.**

Psalm 19; James 4:7-5:6; Mark 9:38-43, 45, 47-48

Kaki Roberts

Proper 22, Sunday Closest to October 5, Year B

Psalm 8. *. . . What are human beings that you are mindful of them, mortals that you care for them?*

I once asked my parents how they managed to stay married for 48 years. Although I asked them separately, they answered in almost exactly the same words: "It was easy. There were hard times, but staying married was easy." They spoke of love for one another, respect for each other and commitment to each other and to the marriage.

Their answer was a surprise to me. My generation does not stay married. We do not know the definition of the word *commitment*. We live for now. If something does not meet our current need, we cast it off and look for something else.

God became human and lived among us to show His commitment to us, His love for us. He asks that we live our lives for Him, to Him, with Him, by Him and in Him. We ask for this sanctification each time we are present at the Eucharist. His Real Presence is there, reminding us that He came to be "a merciful and faithful high priest in the service of God, to make expiation for the sins of the people. For because He Himself has suffered and been tempted, He is able to help those who are tempted."

God will meet our current needs, long-term needs, forever needs—if we will only turn to Him and make the commitment to Him as He made to us before we were ever born.

**This week reflect on God's commitment to you
and your response.**

Genesis 2:18-24; Hebrews 2:1-18; Mark 10:2-9

Kaki Roberts

Proper 23, Sunday Closest to October 12, Year B

Amos 5:6-7, 10-15. *Seek good, not evil—and the Lord Almighty will be with you, just as you say He is.*

After reading this passage, I began to think about all the negative and derogatory comments and insinuations being made daily via newspapers and television regarding our president and several other public officials. Is it the "American way" to always search for the wrong rather than the right? What a better world this would be if we were more mindful of our Lord's example to us and we searched for the good in one another versus the evil!

Upon rereading this passage, it spoke to me directly. Last year I resigned my teaching position because of difficult working relations with my employer. My choice—but I was in pain and angry. After some reflection, I find I have held on to my hurt and anger. I have focused on the wrong and at times even enjoyed hearing negative remarks about my former employer's actions. She had spoken unkindly toward me; so doesn't she deserve it?

This passage in Amos reminds me that my response is not what our Lord desires. In harboring these feelings, I punished myself.

Jesus came to put us right with God. Jesus is good, and when we seek Jesus and allow Him to be the center of our lives and the source of all we think and do, we will truly understand and experience the true meaning of the words, "Seek good, not evil, and the Lord Almighty will be with you."

**Reread this passage and listen as our Lord speaks to you
in areas of your life where you are not seeking good.
Pray for those who have hurt you
and seek the good in them as well as yourself.**

Psalm 90; Mark 10:17-27, (28-31); Hebrews 3:1-6

Kaki Yarborough

Proper 24, Sunday Closest to October 19, Year B

Mark 10:35-45. *For even the Son of Man did not come to be served, but to serve and to give His life a ransom for many.*

No fancy words; no hidden message; just simply stated—Jesus came to serve and give.

Is your perception of the word *servant* negative? Does it cause you to think of someone who is often mistreated or enslaved to others?

Today as you read this passage in Mark's gospel, take heed as to what God says to us about authentic servanthood. Usually we tend to want to get as much out of life as we can, often at the expense of others. However, our real joy comes only from giving more and serving others without expecting anything in return.

Jesus used all of His energies and powers to serve others and in the end, gave His life. By developing an attitude of service, we will begin to see many opportunities to serve others. As servants reach out to one another, we are serving Jesus. Read the following words to "The Servant Song":*

> Brother let me be your servant
> Let me be as Christ to you
> Pray that I may have the grace to let you be my servant
> too.
>
> We are pilgrims on a journey
> We are brothers on the road
> We are here to help each other
> Walk the mile and bear the load.

Pray for strength to follow Jesus' example of loving and caring for others.

Psalm 91; Hebrews 4:12-16; Isaiah 53:4-12

Kaki Yarborough

* *Cry Hosanna*, Gillard, p. 117

Proper 25, Sunday Closest to October 26, Year B

Isaiah 59:(1-4), 9-19. *Rather, your iniquities have been barriers between you and your God, and your sins have hidden His face from you. . . . We wait for light, and lo! There is darkness.*

How do you comfort someone in the despair of the dark night of the soul? It is so awful, so painful. When you are in it, it is difficult to know or feel any reason. Only when I am out of it can I look back and see what has happened.

These are emptying times—times when my life has become filled with something that no longer works. To get out of the "hole," I must shed some baggage, some part of myself, some character defect which has taken over. This shedding is so painful. It is like removing scales to be changed from a dragon back into a boy as happened to Eustace in C. S. Lewis' *Voyage of the Dawn Treader.* One solution is to "deaden" or "ignore" the pain by using our "drug of choice": food, alcohol, power, work or relationships. Another solution is to stay "in the pool," ride the storm, often surrounded or held up only by the love of friends we allow to walk or swim or lie beside us.

We cannot on our own power remove the defects. Our job is to recognize our defects, confess them, but we must let God remove the scales, just as Aslan did for Eustace. This usually takes time. The scab cannot come off before its "time." We also must stay in the recovery room as long as necessary after this surgery.

What sustains us during this time? Read on in Isaiah to verse 21: "Says the Lord, my spirit that is upon you . . . shall not depart out of your mouth . . . from now on and forever." God promises to be with us if we will only have eyes and ears to see and hear. If we stay with the process, we can come out of the "dark night" a new person, healed by whatever God had to remove surgically during that time of darkness.

Pray for all you know are living in the dark night.
Let them know you walk beside them.

Psalm 13; Hebrews 5:12-6:1, 9-12; Mark 10:46-52

Joanna Seibert

All Saints Day, November 1, Year B

Matthew 5:1-12. *Blessed are the poor in spirit, for theirs is the kingdom of heaven. . . . Blessed are you when people revile you and persecute you and utter all kinds of evil against you falsely on my account. Rejoice and be glad, for your reward is great in heaven, for in the same way they persecuted the prophets who were before you.*

The Greek word for *poor* means literally "beggarly." The "poor in spirit" are those who recognize that they must beg for their spirit from a source beyond themselves. Such people find the kingdom, while those who regard themselves as self-sufficient do not receive the highest gift.

On this day when we remember all the saints who have come before us, we reflect on what it is that makes one a saint anyway. It seems like a goal unattainable; yet, indeed, we all are called to achieve such a goal. Para-doxically, few of the saints we know came to union with God through noble and mighty deeds. Most were common folks like you and me. The one thing we all have in common, though, is the cross. There is, indeed, no way that any person is called *saint* except that they recognized and embraced the suffering that came their way and walked the painful path.

As this scripture says, there is no way that we alone can do this. One of the greatest gifts the "12-step" program has given us is that we admit that we ourselves are powerless and come to believe in a power greater than ourselves. We also come to depend upon other persons to help us when the going gets rough and temptation comes again. Those who have carried their own cross know what it's like and are the very ones willing and able to help us bear our burdens. We are in this world together, and only to-gether can we find meaning and ultimately find God at the center of that meaning.

Pray for those who are struggling with dependency upon drugs, alcohol, relationships. Pray for those who have such low self-esteem that they endure abuse and see it as deserved. Pray that all of us may turn to God and each other in our helplessness.

Psalm 149; Ecclesiasticus 44:1-10, 13-14; Revelation 7:2-4, 9-17

Jo Ann Barker

Proper 26, Sunday Closest to November 2, Year B

Psalm 119:1-16. *Oh, that my ways were made so direct that I might keep your statutes!*

I love the line from today's Collect: "Grace that we may run without stumbling to obtain your heavenly promises." I haven't run without stumbling for many years. Some days I cannot walk without stumbling. I have multiple sclerosis, and my left leg simply does not work well.

It has been almost 14 years since the MS was diagnosed; so today it is simply another part of me. I am quite aware of my limits and of the adjustments to my daily routine that help me to lead a normal life.

Today's psalm was written for me! Having MS has forced me to make my ways more direct. Because fatigue is a major problem, I am careful to conserve my energy. I grant myself a set number of trips up and down our stairs each day. I plan the day to include time for resting.

All this seems terribly self-centered. But consider today's gospel reading—the second commandment: "Love your neighbor as yourself." It is easy to forget that final phrase, spending so much of ourselves caring for others that there is nothing left.

My personal challenge is to follow today's gospel while I remember today's psalm. If I fail in making my ways direct, the careful construction of my day collapses. Being with my 7-year-old son is far more exciting than taking yet one more nap. Staying at home with a stack of videos doesn't hold a candle to tutoring reading at my child's school, attending EFM, volunteering as docent at the Arts Center or singing in St. Mark's choir.

Having multiple sclerosis is a special blessing. Being aware of my limitations allows me to overcome this disability. I do not want to stumble through my life; so I choose to walk, not run, as directly as I can.

Consider your own special needs.
What is your disability, and what special challenges
does it pose for you? Do you love yourself
as you love your neighbor?

Deuteronomy 6:1-9; Hebrews 7:23-28; Mark 12:28-34

Teresa Luneau

Proper 27, Sunday Closest to November 9, Year B

Mark 12:38-44. *As He taught, He said, "Beware of the scribes, who like to walk around in long robes, and to be greeted with respect in the marketplaces, and to have the best seats in the synagogues and places of honor at banquets!"*

Have you seen any of these scribes strutting around town lately? You know them—always dressed "to the nines," with frequent sightings revealed in society columns, with season tickets for all the performing arts. They not only support the best nonprofit organizations, but they are also active in their church, both in tithing and in assuming responsibilities in the life of the church.

So what are they—rather, what are we—doing wrong? Is it a sin to be in the public eye, be successful, or be active in the social scene?

Two simple questions can lead us further. Would God be pleased by what I am doing with my life? In my every work, thought, and action, am I living a Christ-centered life?

No matter how we answer, we must remind ourselves that God's concern lies not in our wardrobes, reputations, support of charities or seats in church. God is interested in our striving to live a God-filled life. He wants to see us struggle and succeed as we work to obey His commandments. Our focus must move from the superficial to the supernatural as we learn to return to God our love, our trust, faith and lives.

**As you go through your week, consider some of your
recent choices—making certain purchases,
deciding whether to attend a social event,
perhaps even thinking about why you chose
certain people as friends. Take time to consider:
are these choices made to the glory of God?**

I Kings 17:8-16; Psalm 146; Hebrews 9:24-28

Teresa Luneau

Proper 28, Sunday Closest to November 16, Year B

Hebrews 10:31-39. *It is a fearful thing to fall into the hands of the living God.*

Scary words—how does one *fall into the hands of the living God*? I admit to a feeling of deep chill in my heart when I have trespassed, in word, thought, or deed, against another and the trespass is made known to me. The awareness that I have not only hurt another, but God also, by my action is a fearful thing. On the other hand, it is also comforting because I am aware of His concern for me, as well as the one who is hurt. It is a time for asking forgiveness.

To feel separated from God because my actions reflect not the person He would have me be is a risk I'd rather not take. To be loved so much that my sin can be set before me, forgiven and healing begun turns my fear, guilt and sense of unworthiness into a stepping stone for growing in the life in Christ.

If to fall into the hands of God is to be forgiven, instructed, strengthened and encouraged to continue living in relationship, I say, "Thanks be to God."

Present yourself each day to the living God
that you may be instructed in the way of forgiveness.

Psalm 16; Daniel 12:1-4a, (5-13); Mark 13:14-23

Dotty Goss

Proper 29, Sunday Closest to November 23, Year B

Psalm 93. *The Lord is King; He has put on splendid apparel.*

The psalms represent some of my most favorite reading in scripture. They so wonderfully reflect the human condition. Humanity's acknowledgment of God the Creator, the magnificence of His work, our dependence on him, with laments and praise in equal doses, our tears and anxieties, our vilification of our enemies—one can always find psalms which mirror our own feelings.

Reading Psalm 93 takes me back to my teen-age years and a trip to Colorado with a stay in the Rockies high above Boulder. I had never seen mountains so impressive, nor distances so mind-boggling. Indeed, God had put on splendid apparel and I was filled with awe. I truly felt this was as close to God as one could ever get. Sitting high above the city under the stars but above the clouds and sometimes lightning and rain showers, I could only drink in His presence in holy silence.

Those moments are still very real to me. Yet in time, it was only a moment, for the return to the valley and reentry into the world had to come. Is not the experience of all mountaintop moments that we are called from our aloneness with God to travel with Him down into the valley? How blessed we are that God sets apart time to be with us but then calls us back to share in His earthly ministry!

Give thanks that God has made us partners with Christ in the quiet and busy times of our lives.

Daniel 7:9-14; Revelation 1:1-8; John 18:33-37; Mark 11:1-11

Dotty Goss

Between Heaven and Earth—The Communion of Saints

When I was 17 years old, I began dating the man who was later to become my husband and soul mate. Through him I developed a relationship with his grandmother. My husband once described his grandmother as "a presence." A presence she was! She was a woman of deep faith. Prayer was her companion. She had a delightful childlike quality, which made her charming. She held the family in prayer and supported us with the energy of spirit through her prayer. She took a liking to me and I to her. We enjoyed and treasured each other.

As she aged, I became more aware that someday she would not be with me physically. I would say to her, "Mammaw, if you go to heaven before me, will you promise to pray for me?" She would laugh and say that, if she could pray in heaven, she would pray for me. This conversation became a closing ritual between the two of us so that each time we parted, I would make my same request and she would repeat her same response. This went on for years. We would laugh and I would feel comforted.

My request came from many inner sources. I wanted to keep the connection with her after she died. I wondered what life on the "other side" was like. First and foremost, I had some hard-to-verbalize sense that her continuing to pray for me was part of the ground of my being that upheld and sustained me.

Mammaw died a little over a year ago. During that year, I was completely absorbed in building a house. This was not just any house. It was my dream house, literally conceived of in a series of nighttime dreams and shaped largely by an ongoing series of dreams, which aided and guided me much of the way. It was to be a house with a large, open central space for my family to live in together and private space for each person. It was a house with an intimate relationship with nature, a house filled with spirit and love.

As I completed the house, I would regret that Mammaw would not get to see it. One night two months before we moved in, I had a dream that she came in the front door and saw the beautiful staircase and held her hand and arm up in pleasure, pointing to this creative work and taking delight in it.

About a month later, I had gone to bed uncommonly weary with my housebuilding project. I had a dream that I was in a large city with five "missionary types." It was my job to get a hotel room for them. They needed a place to rest. I negotiated with the manager of a hotel. He listened to what I was doing and gave me a key. I went upstairs expecting one room. Instead, I found a suite of rooms. I was ecstatic. I realized that the hotel manager sensed that I was doing what I had been told to do by the spirit and therefore he gave me a suite of rooms rather than the single one I had expected. I realized that the "missionaries" were actually people who had helped me with the house.

About that time, Mammaw appeared in the dream. She was very young and filled with joy and light. She wore white and one half of her body emitted marvelous, white light toward me. I realized that she was transmitting light from heaven to earth. I could feel her going back and forth from heaven to earth. She would look back to heaven and then look to me, back and forth, connecting heaven and earth, transferring energy from heaven to earth, blessing me in general and blessing my housebuilding project. At some point in the dream, I realized she was about to leave to go back to heaven. I started to cry. I didn't want her to go. I made my familiar request, "Mammaw, will you promise you'll pray for me when you go back to heaven?"

She began to laugh. She was amused and bemused with my request. She shook her head. She said, "You don't understand. Where I am, we are in the energy of prayer *all the time*. That is the way it is."

I realized in the dream, as she said this, that prayer on earth is our way of seeking the presence of God. It is a state we click in and out of, without the ability to sustain it. On the other side, the communion of saints supports us, is in prayer for us and surrounds us with this energy at all times because that is the state in which they exist. I believe we are each receiving the benefit of that interaction and we are continuously upheld, blessed and supported.

From our side of reality, we have two opportunities. First, we have the opportunity to become conscious of and thus more fully receive their support. Secondly, we have the opportunity to click into this prayer state off and on throughout our day and our lives. As we seek to practice the presence of God, we are weaving threads of spirit in and out the tiniest areas of our soul and our lives. We are connecting to the blessing and privilege of prayer. We are being fed with spiritual food and feeding others in the process. We are going back and forth between heaven and earth and being blessed as we do this.

Susan Sims Smith

A CLOUD OF WITNESSES

Pan Adams is a mother of three, wife of one and family therapist, who delights in taking risks for God. Pan wrote that after doing these writings she would never again go through the last week of Advent quite the same.

Jacque Alexander has been an Episcopalian all of her adult life. She is a member of St. Margaret's Episcopal Church in Little Rock. This was her first adventure in meditative or interpretive writing. She is a wife and mother of two boys, 6 and 10. She has worked for 16 years as a local governmental official in the court system.

Madge Brown, after 35 years of involvement in Episcopal volunteer work at the diocesan, provincial and national levels, has "retired" to a more selective ministry, focusing on her association with the monastic community of the Holy Spirit, intercessory prayer, varied involvement with St. Michael's mission in Little Rock and work with the homeless through Our House shelter.

Sue Campbell is a psychotherapist in private practice in Little Rock, with 54 years in the Episcopal Church, 32 years as a wife and mother and 10 years of study in Jungian psychology.

Jeanie Carter is a secretary for St. Luke's Episcopal Church/Day School in Hot Springs. Her hobbies are writing poetry (one book) and being a grandmother.

Jo Ann Barker writes that God, her husband and three children and the community of Christians in the Arkansas Diocese have prompted her to realize her vocation to the ordained priesthood. Indeed she has experienced the love and support of being enmeshed in the "cloud of witnesses."

Lida Coyne is a grandmother who lives in a cabin in the woods of North Central Arkansas. She is a member of St. Francis Episcopal Church in Heber Springs. She serves on the secretariat of the Episcopal Cursillo and is active in the Kairos ministry.

Ginger Crisp is an attorney, wife, mother of adult career women and active choir member of St. Paul's, Fayetteville.

Elizabeth Crocker is a mother, grandmother, university administrator and faculty member, transplanted Baptist and active choir member of St. Paul's, Fayetteville.

Patsy Daggett teaches a class called "Innerwork Through Art" at St. Michael's in Little Rock and a class for persons with AIDS at the Arkansas Arts Center. She is a student in clinical pastoral education at the University of Arkansas for Medical Sciences.

Sammye Dewoody is a member of Trinity, Pine Bluff. She has been a parish administrator for 14 years and has worked on various committees for her province, diocese and parish. She has been an active member of the Camp Mitchell board. She is married to Dick and has one daughter, Maggie.

Mary Donovan is a historian, teacher and wife of the Eleventh Bishop of Arkansas.

Sandy Finkbeiner is treasurer of the diocesan Episcopal Church Women. She is a full-time graduate student, working on a master's in business administration at UALR. She has two children—Becki Streett, a part-time math instructor at UALR, and Andrew, a Peace Corps volunteer in Swaziland, Africa.

Anne Fulk teaches an adult discussion class at Christ Church, Little Rock. She is a founding and active board member of Second Genesis, a home for women released and paroled from prison.

Ann R. Gornatti is a housewife, mother and recent grandmother. She is a cradle Episcopalian, member of Al-Anon and graduate of Education for Ministry. She no longer believes in our "just" rewards but is grateful for God's mercy.

Dotty Goss is a grandmother who discovered the joys of the spiritual journey after arriving in the "promised land" (Arkansas) 17 years ago.

Rochelle Graves is a divorced mother of a 7-year-old daughter. Her "spare" time includes church, PTA, Girl Scouts and pursuing a degree in business administration.

Ann Grimes is the mother of two sons—one in college and one in high school. After teaching for 12 years, divorcing and marrying again, she began law school at age 39. She is in her fourth year as clerk for a state judge.

Deb Halter is a former editor for the *Arkansas Catholic*. She works in communications and public relations at Arkansas Children's Hospital and writes a weekly column for the *Arkansas Democrat-Gazette*.

Joyce Hardy is a deacon at St. Margaret's and director of Summer Celebration, a program for inner-city children in Little Rock.

Peggy Hays is a former psychotherapist who is now an Episcopal priest at St. Peter's, Conway.

Merry Helen Hedges is a deacon at St. Michael's, Little Rock, and director of pastoral care at Presbyterian Village.

Scottie Healy is an assistant professor of teacher education at UALR. She is a founding member of St. Margaret's in Little Rock, the wife of Floyd and mother of Catherine and Charles.

Connie Hollenberg is an Episcopalian, gardener, Education for Ministry mentor, wife, mother and grandmother, lover of movies and gypsy in her heart.

Dodi Horne was a writer, editor, medical researcher, licensed massage therapist and mother of two daughters. She died before the publication of her work. Although she struggled bravely with her illness, she wanted to be remembered not for her fight with death but her enthusiam for life.

Claudia Howe is a mother and wife. She lives in West Memphis, Arkansas, with husband John, teaches high-school English and is a licensed social worker. Claudia is a "child of God," and her biblical soul sister is Mary Magdalene.

Jenny Jackson writes that her favorite answer to the question, "Who are you?" comes from an old Loretta Young TV show: "I am a child of God." It is difficult for her to pick out any one part of herself. She enjoys all her roles: wife, mother, St. Margaret's office manager—being a "child of God." As St. Margaret's office manager, she has the opportunity to be intimately involved in the creation and growth of a new church.

Trudy James is director of Regional AIDS Interfaith Network (RAIN) in Arkansas.

Karen Darker Johnson teaches elementary students with learning disabilities and is pursuing a master's degree in that field. In her free time, she enjoys singing in the church choir, reading and directing a session of summer camp at Camp Mitchell.

Nyna Keeton is Christian life coordinator at St. Mark's Church, Little Rock, a lay reader and chalice bearer.

Julie Keller lives in Little Rock, is editor of the *Arkansas Episcopalian,* is married to Christoph Keller, the vicar of St. Margaret's, and has two children, Christoph and Mary Olive.

Mary Kumpuris is a wife and mother of three. She lives in Little Rock and is a member of St. Mark's Episcopal Church and graduate of Education for Ministry.

Virginia Kutait is a member of St. Bartholomew's, Fort Smith. She wrote about her experience of writing her meditations: "I was forced to examine the unfamiliar."

Teresa Luneau is a Little Rock native and member of St. Mark's. She is a writer and works on assignments for national publications. She taught English, world literature and English as a second language for nine years at the University of Arkansas at Fayetteville and Little Rock. She has a son, Patrick. Her husband Harold is an administrator at UALR.

Andrea McMillin is a recent graduate of Yale Divinity School.

Dean McMillin is a mother of four daughters and has four grandchildren. She is married to Tom and is a lifelong resident of Little Rock. She has been a member of St. Mark's for 32 years. She started and managed The Bookmark store for 11 years. She currently is developing and directing a training program to prepare citizens for community service within local agencies in Arkansas, Louisiana and Mississippi.

Karen McClard attends church at St. Luke's, North Little Rock, and is active in the Episcopal Church Women.

Susan May is a walker, hiker, traveler, yogi, Education for Ministry graduate, volunteer, wife and mother.

Joanne Meadors lives in Little Rock and wants to be remembered by us as a pilgrim.

Deb Meisch lives with her husband in Fayetteville, where she is a member of St. Paul's Episcopal Church and is active at St. Martin's Episcopal University Center. She is an instructor in the Communications Department at the University of Arkansas. When she's not teaching, researching or spending time with her family, she likes to hike, fish and canoe.

Starr Mitchell is a musician, mother of two boys, wife to George and a member of St. Margaret's. She works with the Arkansas Territorial Restoration.

Virginia Mitchell wrote her meditations in her 80th year. She has three daughters, one son, nine grandchildren and one great-grandchild. She is widow of William Starr Mitchell, who was chancellor of the Diocese of Arkansas for 18 years. She was a faithful member of Trinity Cathedral until she had the "irresistible call" to start a new church three years ago. She is one of the 28 missionary members of St. Margaret's Episcopal Church.

Sydney Murphy is a designer in El Dorado and is very active in the Cursillo movement.

Mary Janet "Bean" Murray is a member of St. Michael's, Little Rock. She made her Cursillo at 42 and was on the team for Arkansas Cursillo at 46. She is in her second year of Education for Ministry. She is the advocacy supervisor at the Arkansas Department of Human Services Division of Aging and Adult Services. She is wife to Paul and mother to Cara, 18, and Chris, 14.

Susan Payne is a seminarian at Seabury-Western Theological Seminary.

Diane Plunkett lives in North Little Rock with her husband and 16-year-old daughter. She also has a son in college. She works part-time in a preschool nursery, taking care of babies, her favorite of God's creatures.

Suzanne Pyron is a practicing dental hygienist who lives in Hot Springs with her husband Than, two children, Mary Tully and Stacy Rebekah Pyron, and her grandmother, Mary Stacy Flood.

Phyllis Raney is a psychotherapist in private practice in Little Rock. She describes her practice as working with people who want to build lasting relationships and enhance the quality of their lives through personal growth. She is the mother of two grown sons, on the program council of the Oasis Renewal Center and member of St. Margaret's Episcopal Church.

Jane Roark is a registered nurse practitioner, teacher and consultant in Little Rock. She was born in Toronto, Canada, and spent her first 11 years in the Anglican Church.

Kaki Roberts wrote that she could not tell when she was hearing God's word and when she was putting God's word in His mouth. She prayed that somewhere in her meditations was God's word. She wrote her meditations at Hesychia House of Prayer. What resulted was a surprise to her. She works in the office of Julia Hughes Jones in Little Rock and is active in Cursillo and the Episcopal Church Women.

Beverly Roth is a member of St. Mark's, Hope. She is married, has three girls, works with disabled people and is active in Cursillo and the Kairos prison ministry.

Betty Rowland is a charter member of St. Mark's, Little Rock, former editor of the *Arkansas Episcopalian* (then known as *The Churchman*) and writer of skits and parodies for all occasions.

Charliss Russ is single, 41 years old and a newly confirmed Episcopalian. Five and one-half years ago, she became a Big Sister volunteer to Tracy. " I cannot begin to describe how the Heavenly Father has enriched my life since then. I truly feel loved," she wrote.

Joanna Seibert is a radiologist at Arkansas Children's Hospital, mother of three grown children, Robert, John and Joanna, and wife of Robert.

Susan Sims Smith is a psychotherapist, workshop leader and teacher, who seeks to integrate her Christian faith with a Jungian approach to psychological and spiritual growth. She lives with her husband Rick and daughter, Rose, in Little Rock and is a member of St. Margaret's.

Caroline Sneed is a long-time member of St. Michael's, Little Rock. She is active within the Arkansas Alliance for the Mentally Ill and the National Alliance and is coordinator for the Episcopal Mental Illness Network.

Pam Strickland is a journalist and writer. She lives in Little Rock with Theo, the wonder dog.

Robin Sudderth is a member of St. Mark's, Little Rock.

Becky Tucker is a wife, mother and law student in Little Rock.

Linda Walker is a member of St. Mark's, Little Rock, wife to Brent and mother to Noah and Sarah.

Mary Ware is a native Arkansan, retired from the Arkansas Teacher Retirement System and an active Episcopalian in Cursillo, Education for Ministry, vestry and RAIN teams. She recently moved from Little Rock to Conway and consequently from St. Michael's to St. Peter's.

Julia Wepfer was taught the prayer discipline she uses in her meditation by Jane Wolfe at Trinity Episcopal Cathedral. She has used this discipline 11 years. She meets once a week with a group which shares aloud what each has written. Julia is a mother and is retired as faculty member of the University of Arkansas for Medical Sciences Department of Psychiatry. She has a psychotherapy practice at home.

Elaine Williams is the mother of two, wife of one, editor for the Agricultural Experiment Station and 15-year resident of Arkansas. Much of her fellowship and spiritual struggle happens within the community of St. Paul's, Fayetteville, for which she is most grateful.

Sandra Wheat is a scientist in public health. Previously she was active in Cursillo, teaching Sunday school, Thebe and lay reading. Currently she is in prayer to see what God wants for her next "passage."

Gay White is passionate about the outdoors and experiences it through hiking and canoeing. She enjoys "connecting" with other women who are seeking God and sharing her experience, strength and hope, as well as receiving encouragement from them.

Kaki Yarborough, a former school teacher, is mother of two children and wife of the rector of Christ Church, Little Rock. She has one delightful granddaughter, Molly, and loves being a grandmother.

Ann Young is a Presbyterian minister, retreat director, psychotherapist, spiritual director and sometime writer living in Little Rock. She has a special interest in the relationship between psychology and spirituality, transformation and human wholeness. She enjoys working with myths and fairy tales as metaphors for the spiritual journey.

Artist's Note

I am currently studying religion at Yale Divinity School, and I will return to Little Rock in May 1994 to live with my husband, who is in medical school. During the summer of 1992, I discovered that my true art medium is pottery, and the shapes in my drawings reflect that. I also love to paint and draw.

This project has been exciting and enriching for me in many ways. It opened up a part of me that has been dormant for several years. While in school, my work centers around words: in books, lectures, conversations, papers. There is little time for expressing myself with images, although they are constant companions to me.

During the course of this project, my hands remembered much of the pleasure I find in drawing. I also remembered what it is like to struggle and fight to get what is in my head and heart out on paper. That is so difficult for me. When I was a child, I would throw the pencil across the room and cry out in frustration because my imaginings could not be transferred to paper.

As I worked on these drawings, there were some frustrating days when I was sure that this work was pointless. This time I found that if I prayed for the presence of the Holy Spirit, I would gain the strength to work through the periods of anger and frustration. The only way out of the anger is through it, I've found, and it is exciting to find God there in the midst of that turmoil, as well as in the peace.

Andrea McMillin

How to Order

Please send _____ copies of *Surrounded by a Cloud of Witnesses.*

I am enclosing a check for $_____.

SURROUNDED BY A CLOUD OF WITNESSES:
Publication Price: $13.95

Name _____

Address _____

City _____ State _____ Zip _____

Fill out this order blank and send check to:
Episcopal Church Women of Diocese of Arkansas, c/o Teresa Luneau,
9913 Echo Valley Ct., Little Rock, AR 72227